I0120892

—GENEALOGY—
How to Find Your Ancestors

REVISED EDITION

Paul Drake, J.D. and Margaret Grove Driskill

HERITAGE BOOKS
2012

HERITAGE BOOKS

AN IMPRINT OF HERITAGE BOOKS, INC.

Books, CDs, and more—Worldwide

For our listing of thousands of titles see our website
at
www.HeritageBooks.com

Published 2012 by
HERITAGE BOOKS, INC.
Publishing Division
100 Railroad Ave. #104
Westminster, Maryland 21157

Copyright © 2000 Paul Drake and Margaret Grove Driskill

Prior to revision, portions of this book were previously published in *In Search of Family History: A Starting Place.*

Cover photograph: George Washington Lankford (b. 1856) and Laura Emmaline Myers
Lankford (b. 1858), maternal great-grandparents of co-author Margaret Grove Driskill.

Other Heritage Books by Paul Drake and Margaret Grove Driskill:

Genealogy: How to Find Your Ancestors, Revised Edition
Paul Drake, J.D. and Margaret Grove Driskill

Other Heritage Books by Paul Drake:

*CD: Now in Our Fourth Century: Some American Families: A Documentary and
Pictorial History of More Than Twenty Families Who Were Well Settled
in the American Colonies Before the Year 1700*

In Search of Family History: A Starting Place

*Missing Pieces: How to Find Birth Parents and Adopted Children
A Search and Reunion Guidebook*
Paul Drake and Beth Sherrill

More What Did They Mean by That

Now in Our Fourth Century: Some American Families

*What Did They Mean By That? A Dictionary of Historical
and Genealogical Terms, Old and New*

*What Did They Mean By That? A Dictionary of Historical
Terms for Genealogists: Some More Words, Volume 2*

What Did They Mean by That? A Dictionary of Historical Terms for Genealogists

*You Ought to Write All That Down: A Guide to Organizing
and Writing Genealogical Narrative*

*You Ought to Write All That Down: A Guide to Organizing
and Writing Genealogical Narrative, Revised Edition*

All rights reserved. No part of this book may be reproduced or transmitted in any form or by any means,
electronic or mechanical, including photocopying, recording or by any information storage and retrieval system
without written permission from the author, except for the inclusion of brief quotations in a review.

International Standard Book Numbers
Paperbound: 978-0-7884-1476-3
Clothbound: 978-0-7884-9281-5

Table of Contents

List of Illustrations.. *vii*

Acknowledgments.. *ix*

Introduction... *xi*

Chapter 1 ***Thoughts on Starting*** 1

Starting the Search 1
Evidence and Proof 3
Measures of Evidence.. 5

Chapter 2 ***Interviews, Veterans, Churches & Cemeteries*** 7

The Importance of Maps... 7
Sensitive Areas of Discussion 9
Commencing the Interview 9
Techniques for Jogging the Memory.. 11
Keeping Control of the Interview 13
Additional Questions... 13
Veterans.. 15
The National Archives and Veterans' Records............................ 15
Veterans' Records in Libraries and Archives.............................. 19
Societies and Clubs 22
Churches... 23
Cemeteries.. 24

Chapter 3 ***The Internet*** 27

What Can Be Found.. 27
Volunteer Projects.. 29
Records of the States of the Union 30
Latter Day Saints 31
Historic Photographs.. 32

Chapter 4 ***Libraries*** 33

Commencing Your Library Research 33
Changing Boundaries.. 33
Books.. 37

Citing Sources 37
Searching For An Ancestor 38
Censuses 39
Interpreting Census Records 41
Moving Backwards In Time 42
Reliability of Census Information 43
Illiteracy 44
Other Factors Causing Errors 44
Boarders and Live-ins 44
Origins of Surnames 45
The Spelling of Names 45
Cousins and "Greats" 46
Birth, Adoptive and Foster Parents 47
Titles and Forms of Address 47
Researching Through the Use of Ages 47
Time Line Drawings 48
Departments of Vital Statistics 49
Genealogical Clubs and Societies 51
Local Materials 52
Genealogical Periodicals 54
Indentured Servants, Redemptioners and Criminals 55
Passenger Lists 56
Looking Abroad 56
Using Library Catalogs 57
Migration Routes 59
Summary 60

Chapter 5 **Courthouses** 61

Starting Courthouse Research 62
Maps 64
Legal Terms 65
Deeds 65
Mortgages 67
Warranty Deeds 69
Marriages, Children and Deaths 69
Quit-Claims 70
Deeds of Partition 72
Considerations in Deeds 72
Locating Real Estate 74
Probate Records 74
Estates 75
Testate Death Proceedings 75
Intestate Death Proceedings 77
Bonds, Inventories, Appraisements and Sales 77
Lawsuits and Other Court Activities 79
Reading Early English 80
Loose Papers 82

Naturalization Records 83
Tax Records 83
Good Genealogy Manners 86
Care of Records 86
Writing About Your Family 86

Conclusion 91

Appendix 1 **Forms** 93
Pedigree Chart (horizontal format) 94
Pedigree Chart (vertical format) 95
Family Unit Chart 96
Census Forms:
1790 Census 97
1800-1810 Census 98
1820 Census 99
1830-1840 Census 100
1850 Census 101
1860 Census 102
1870 Census 103
1880 Census 104
1900 Census 105
1910 Census 106
1920 Census 107

Appendix 2 **The National Archives** 109
National Archives Regional Archives System 111

Appendix 3 **Societies, Periodicals, Directories and Miscellaneous Agencies** 113
Societies 113
Periodicals 114
Directories 114
Miscellaneous Agencies 114

Glossary 115

Index 129

About the Authors 141

List of Illustrations

U.S.G.S. Quadrangle, or topographical map 8
Probate court record: Statement of insanity 10
1927 Automobile registration 12
Photograph of ancestor standing beside train 14
Revolutionary War-era document 18
Widow's Pension from National Archives 20
Civil War-era military medical discharge document 21
English baptismal record dated 1647 23
Mourning Card dated 1890 25
Deed dated 1741/1742 28
Well-drawn map from *Atlas of Wyandot Co., Ohio* 36
Death Certificate dated 1956 50
1810 list of resident tax-payers found in a county history 53
Landowner map of Madison Township, 1871 54
1723 Virginia petition with names of area residents 60
1904 Marriage License 63
Certified copy of a 1760 document 66
1773 Marriage Bond 71
Typical deed to be found in all courthouses 73
Inventory and appraisal of 1760s estate 78
1698 Will: An example of an old document that is difficult to read 81
Example of Loose Papers: Swearing-in of constables in 1755 82
Example of Loose Papers: List of Tithables, or taxable citizens, 1755 84
Obituary notice from 1827 newspaper 88
Sketch of ancestral home from Civil War book 89
Photograph of President Lincoln with ancestral home in background............ 90

Acknowledgments

This effort is dedicated to the students who, through requiring me to truly consider whereof I spoke, brought a level of understanding of the subject which otherwise I would not have acquired; to dear Margaret for her assistance, patience, and wonderful contributions, without which this effort at revision would have added but precious little; to Paul R. (and again Margaret), for his many hours spent and knowledge added concerning what to me were very new tools—the computer and the Internet; to Paul again, and to Diane and Cheryl, who over these years have granted to me the encouragement and inspiration to continue in this and all research efforts; to dearest little Brittany, Bethany, Evan, Diane, Allison, Mikaila and Drake, and their yet unnamed descendants for being my wonderful grandchildren; to James Houston and Debbie Hall at the library for their time and assistance; to Roxanne Carlson for her patience and help on a thousand occasions; to Gerald Haynes for his unending willingness to help with illustrations; and to Marty for often doing what should have been my chores to do. I sincerely love and thank every one of you. -P.D.

My heartfelt appreciation to my sister Helen, the true Historian in our family. Her lifetime search for "dead people" finally became contagious for her baby sister. All that I do, or will ever do, is for the pride of my grandchildren, Sean, Megan, Derek and Harrison. God bless you all. -M.G.D.

Introduction

It is our sincere hope that this handbook will serve as a guide as you begin your journey through family research. All of the following suggestions have been tried and tested many times before, and while there will be no genealogy policeman come by if you don't apply the suggestions made here, we think you will be well served if you do.

You will find it desirable to do interviews of relatives, to go to communities where ancestors once lived, to visit cemeteries where they now rest, and to organize what you have learned from those sources and from family tales and traditions. Then you will want to visit libraries and courthouses and add all that you can. You may want to take a course, join a society, do some writing, contribute time and materials to others and to publications, submit queries and research findings, and to ask questions of all who will answer. All the while you will be meeting some of the nicest people in the world.

Then too, many of these nice people are involved in their own research on the World Wide Web (WWW). If you are connected to the Internet, you will find there many sources of information that you can and will want to use. During the course of our study, we will guide you to many of these, and it is likely that you will find others who are hunting for the same surname as are you.

Of this be sure; you and those who come after you will be proud of your ancestors and of their triumphs and even their failures and will be equally proud of your work in uncovering evidence of their lives. As a result of your search, instead of remaining as mere names and dates in a family Bible, those long dead will become living, breathing human beings.

Every one of your ancestors has stories to tell, and you will come to fully understand that the emotions and feelings experienced by you were well known to those who went before. They will surprise you and eloquently speak out to you at every turn. Perhaps most of all, and to your distinct benefit, through knowledge of those who long ago traveled this road, you will come face to face with your own mortality.

In a beautiful old country cemetery in Ohio there is the grave of a Welsh lady who died many years before our Civil War. Her tombstone reads:

> *Remember Friend, as you pass by*
> *What you are today, so once was I*
> *What I am now, you will be*
> *So prepare yourself to follow me.*

Good luck in your search.

1

Thoughts on Starting

Almost all persons who have lived within the last four hundred years have left some evidence of their lives, and the search for these records can provide a delightful and inexpensive hobby. There are many sources of information, many places to go looking, and, for the most part, the search is easy. Further, since the records of past events change but very little with the passage of time, when other obligations demand it, the study of family history may be put aside for long periods and then recommenced with ease.

The famous and great names of history—George Washington, Queen Elizabeth I, Ben Franklin, General Lee, and the others—left their marks in many places. For the most part, however, your ancestors were common men and women and for that reason will be somewhat more difficult to locate. Still though, the lives of common folks are every bit as interesting as are those of the wealthy and prominent, and, after all, in physical makeup and even in the way you think, speak, act, and eat, you are the genetic, cultural, and social product of each and every one of those ancestors, rich or poor, gentle or low born as they may have been. What's more, finding a pirate or a thief among your ancestors will only add to the excitement of your discoveries.

Surely too, and most importantly, those who went before deserve better than to be reduced to the mere impersonal dates of their births, marriages, and deaths. It follows that while the gathering of dates is important and perhaps interesting, that effort is but a small part of the total task. Once gathered, we must arrange and interpret the materials uncovered in the context of the events—the history—of that earlier time and place, and so bring to life those who went before. In doing this, you will come to realize that most of those joys, sorrows, pains, and pleasures that you feel were known equally by your ancestors.

Starting The Search

So, how do you commence? Where do you start? First off, inquire at the local library or museum concerning genealogy courses being offered in your area. Many night courses in family research are available for modest sums, and you should make every effort to enroll in one of them. They are very helpful and will provide you with guidance, assistance, and with new friends who share your interests. Even if you have been doing research for years, advanced courses will be most useful to you.

That done, the next step is to plan to keep complete records. Note taking is an absolute necessity in research, since once you have begun to uncover facts and details about your family these must be recorded and saved. In addition to notes, over the years many different printed forms have been devised by other researchers who had the same organizational problems that you will encounter. Several of the most common forms are included in the appendices at the end of this handbook, and nearly all genealogy associations, genealogical bookstores, and libraries have additional inexpensive forms for other family research uses.

Of the forms, perhaps the most often used is the *family unit chart* (also called a *family group sheet*, see Appendix 1), which focuses on an individual and his or her spouse and their children. These forms provide space in which to list numerous facts concerning their lives and those of their parents and children as well, all to be noted with the appropriate dates and sources. A three ring binder, such as may be procured in the school supply section of most any department store, is a convenient way to keep these and other forms. You should organize all forms in alphabetical order by surname (last name).

At once, you should commence filling out and place in your binder a family unit chart for each and every marriage that you come upon. Also in the binder, and immediately following that family unit (or group) chart, you should have a sheet or two of lined paper for your future notes concerning the people within that family unit. This simple combination—along with the census forms mentioned below and included herein—will serve nearly all your organizational needs.

Also provided in Appendix 1 is what is called a *five-generation pedigree chart*. It will provide an overall perspective of the last few generations of your family, from which vantage point you can move forward with your search. The pedigrees provide space for a minimum of information concerning you, your parents, their parents, etc., back to and including your great-great grandparents. It is suggested that you now fill in that form as completely as possible. Remember however, even when the pedigree form is totally completed, you will not have finished your research, you will have only commenced it. As said, genealogy is the study of family history, not a gathering of names and dates.

Of major importance are the forms for recording information gained from the various federal *Decennial Censuses* (every ten years), again included in Appendix 1. As you will here learn, censuses provide vital clues and data, and as with all other information, your findings from these sources must be recorded in an understandable fashion.

Before you start, you should know that you will not find all of your people. Many ancestors will remain hidden for years, and some will never be uncovered. Know too that the frustration of being unable to link two people or to find a parent of some ancestor has been experienced by all who love this hobby. Still though, never decide that there is no point in looking further; as if by magic, ancestors sometimes appear when we least expect it. One day you might be reading an e-mail from someone on a surname list, and BINGO, they have just written about someone you have been looking for and did not think you would ever find.

Now, as you commence and forever more, make a firm resolution that you will not guess and then presume a fact to be true; that you will not assume a kinship simply because it seems apparent and you have looked long and hard; that you will not represent to others that a relationship is likely if, in fact, you are not really sure yourself; and that you will not wish strange parents upon your ancestors. In short, if you are unable to prove a relationship, resolve now that you will not pretend, even to yourself, that you have done so.

Evidence and Proof

Genealogy may be defined as the gathering, organization, consideration, and setting forth of facts and states of being concerning lineage. Accordingly, it is necessary that you now think a bit about evidence and proof.

You must carefully consider what tests and standards must be met before you may accept this or that accumulation of evidence as proof of some relationship. First off, always remember that speculation, conjecture, and guesses are NOT evidence, and evidence is not proof. Evidence consists of facts, states of being, and words. The existence of a gravestone or a war medal are *facts;* these and their total surroundings—their context—are *states of being;* and the spoken or written materials concerning both are *words*. All three support this or that supposition and provide evidence to be interpreted by you. So too is a family tradition told to you by your grandmother, an entry in a Bible or a newspaper, a military discharge kept by a relative, or a recorded deed signed by an ancestor. Conversely, a guess or speculation by some cousin that an ancestor "must have" come from here or there because it makes "good sense" and he or she never heard anything different are not evidence and may not be used as proof of anything. Directions to follow in future research, maybe; evidence, not at all.

Being determined to accept only sufficient evidence as proof does not mean that you can not enjoy what a new-found cousin might have to say about your family. While you are learning what your ancestors did and why they did it, you can—and should—enjoy such stories and have fun, as well. Remember that genealogy is a delightful hobby, not a weary collection of facts. You are searching for heart beats, not just names and dates.

While the answers are not simple, the questions to ask yourself each time you discover a new bit of evidence may be easily stated: Does this evidence speak directly to the question you are trying to answer, or, instead, is it but indirect evidence concerning that question? Should you rely on this source, or should you look for a better and more reliable source of the same information? How much weight should be given this bit of factual material or, for that matter, any other evidence learned from a source such as this one? Stated still another way, what is the value of this evidentiary discovery? A few examples will suffice for this study.

The genealogist has not been born who can state the value (or lack of it) of any bit of evidence without first knowing what it is that we seek to prove with that offering. Why so? Because, all evidence varies greatly as to the weight it should be given (its *probative value*), depending entirely upon what question is being asked. Even a simple entry in an old family Bible varies greatly in its value depending on what we seek to prove with it. As an example, the name and date of birth of a child in a Bible probably is quite reliable as to the name of that child (usually that fact would be clear in the mind of one who undertook to write the entry), is somewhat less reliable as to the precise date of the birth (the entry may have been written by other than a parent and probably was made some days or weeks later), may be even still less credible as to the importance of religion in that family (most everyone owned a Bible, then and now), and remains almost without value in determining what became of that child in later life. So, to say flatly that Bible entries are reliable or not so is to ignore the possibilities.

Then too, consider a military discharge. It is almost surely reliable as to the name of the regiment or unit in which the soldier served, yet is almost valueless as it relates to the bravery of the soldier (even though, since he was honorably discharged, it is clear that he was not a total coward). It is equally lacking in value in showing his attitudes toward war in general (many was the soldier who went to war only because he was required so to do), and it tells us virtually nothing as to the question of who were his parents or children. So, ask yourself, does the evidence before me speak directly to the question that I am trying to answer or, if I use this evidence, must I infer something not really written here? Notice; a discharge expressly states the name of a soldier and his military unit, yet you must infer his patriotism.

As another example, think about a headstone among many in a churchyard. That state of being is almost proof positive that under that stone lies a person of that name (notice, we said "almost"), is somewhat less persuasive as to the dates carved on the stone (most likely that information was placed there weeks, even months, after the death of the person buried there), is still less reliable as to the relationship of the dead person to others with the same surname buried nearby (especially if the name was a common one), is surely quite unreliable if the question is whether or not the dead person attended services at that church (he may have died in a saloon fight or in prison, for all we know, and was buried there through his mother's influence with the pastor), and is really nearly valueless if we seek to learn of the character or personality of that person (even though, still, we may make some tentative assumptions based on his presence in that geographical area). Remember too, that quite probably the deceased did not buy the headstone.

A family tale or tradition is often quite reliable concerning the names of the persons involved and where they were at the time of the incident being related, yet is very much less believable concerning the dates, numbers, and exact words of the people involved. Books are only as reliable as are their authors, and are only quotable as authority and proof insofar as the author personally experienced the events or specified the original sources from which he or she gained the information stated. If you would not be persuaded were the author speaking the words directly to you, then do not believe his or her writings. Note here that a novel, no matter how well researched and enjoyable to read, may not be quoted as proof of anything.

Many are the sources that must be used with caution and a generous measure of skepticism. Always look closely at the source of every fact or relationship, and earnestly ask yourself whether or not the evidence before you is the best available means by which to prove your point. If it is not, you must find the better source. Your genealogical research work is believable and has value only insofar as you have done a thorough job in seeking out and evaluating the best available evidence. A copy of a deed showing ownership is vastly more reliable (and believable) than a memory of a relative stating that same ownership. Your recollection of the given name of a grandfather is far less reliable than his mother's Bible entry stating that fact.

A word concerning sources from which genealogical evidence comes is appropriate. Some writers have undertaken to divide genealogical and historical materials into two categories; one they call *primary sources*, which category supposedly includes only those bits of evidence, artifacts, and writings that were done or created at or near the time of the event being recorded or were written or performed by a person or persons who either was a participant or surely had knowledge concerning the subject matter, or both. The other category they call *secondary sources*. This latter group is said to include all evidence that is derived, or abstracted from, or in some manner grows out of the primary materials.

Though of very little value to researchers, such categorizations are easy in the extreme. It is easy to see that we might label the handwritten dispatches of General Lee at Gettysburg as "primary." Equally, someone's 1985 writings concerning Lincoln's thoughts near the Grove House at Antietam surely could be labeled as "secondary" under the definitions given above. But how would we categorize a veteran's recollections written fifty years later concerning the heroic actions of another person who also was there? We cannot. And if we could, how would it benefit us? Do we know any more or are we more able to use such facts because we label them as "primary" or "secondary" or something else still? We don't think so.

A deed is probably more reliable than a newspaper article showing the same ownership, yet both are evidence, and both are vital to the researcher. A *birth certificate* signed by the attending physician (even though often containing errors) is probably more dependable than a Bible entry written days or weeks after that blessed event, nevertheless both tend to establish the fact of birth and must be carefully noted. An article in the Wall Street Journal relating that an ancestor was involved in a lawsuit is more reliable than a similar article in the gossip papers found at the supermarket check-out, yet both are much less reliable than the record of the court clerk where the lawsuit was filed.

Whether the reliability of a source is great or small, as a researcher you must gather and consider all sources. Ignore all labels, and throughout the course of your searching examine all evidence, no matter how it is described or spoken of by others. Make your own honest decisions concerning reliability and the weight to be given information based solely upon your experience and sound judgment.

Measures of Evidence

Genealogical proof is nothing more (nor less) than the accumulation of that quantity of evidence—those bits of evidentiary material and facts—sufficient to convince a knowledgeable, diligent, and conscientious researcher that some relationship is established. "Convince" is the tricky word here, and what would convince one person might come nowhere close to doing so in the view of someone else. Because of that difficulty, genealogists (and historians) have long struggled with definitions, and the result often has been to state that lineage must be proved by a preponderance of evidence or that it must be of such a nature as to be clear and convincing to all. Despite those diligent efforts, both measures are so subjective as to be of almost no help, especially to the beginner.

So, how should you resolve the question? In the last analysis, it is our intellectual honesty and integrity which control and demand that the accumulation of evidence be of such clarity and forcefulness that the researcher feels no embarrassment or lack of confidence in relating the findings to anyone in the genealogical community. Said another way; before lineage may be said to be established, there should be evidence of such weight and value that if nothing clearly to the contrary is presented a reasonable and intelligent person will consider the matter decided.

Enough of labels, evidence, and proof for now. The careful reader will learn as we go. So what do we do and where do we commence our search? There are four (4) major categories of available sources. The first category is called by us *Interviews, Veterans, Churches, and Cemeteries.*

2

Interviews, Veterans, Churches & Cemeteries

Living memories gained through interviews provide easily accessible facts and directions to many other facts, and most family researchers by no means have fully utilized the information that may be uncovered simply by questioning others. You must—repeat, MUST—talk to and gain all that may be learned from those relatives yet living who share common ancestors with you, especially the eldest ones. Countless times, a family researcher has gained a new fact from a member of another branch of the family whose recollections included information passed down through only their line. Remember that upon the death of such relatives their knowledge will be lost forever, and to uncover even a small part of what those folks have stored in their minds would take years of research. Indeed, most such facts could and would never be found.

So, you have arranged a meeting with a relative. Now what? Along with your three-ring binder and forms, if at all possible, take with you a tape or cassette recorder. As with the rest of us, your memory simply is not good enough to store all of the information you are about to gain. If a recorder is not available despite your best efforts, be prepared to write down ALL answers given, the same to be used for later comparison with your other notes. It also is very important that you take your camera, and if you have one, also take with you a map of the area.

The Importance of Maps

If you do not have a map, simply call or drop in at the office of the county engineer or of any surveyor in the area of your search. They will either have inexpensive maps or will direct you to someone locally who does. Then too, you might ask at the local Chamber of Commerce. Oftentimes they have good area maps. Later, when you have established the precise neighborhood where an ancestor and his family made their home, you will want a more detailed map of that area. For that purpose, the best are the *U. S. Geological Survey 7.5-minute quadrangles*, called by most folks *topos* or *quads*. Such maps are inexpensive, very accurate and highly detailed, and show hills and mountains, streams, swamps, vegetation, cities and towns, roads, rural houses and buildings, many cemeteries, notations of historical sites, and much other information important to the genealogist. Often, the same county engineer, tax office, or Chamber of Commerce will stock such topos. If you already know the precise area you will need, and want to solve the map problem ahead of time, you may write to the U. S. Geological Survey, Washington, D.C., and ask for a list of 7.5' USGS quadrangles for those approximate areas in which you will be searching. These maps also may be procured from the government by the use of your credit card at 1-800-USA-MAPS.

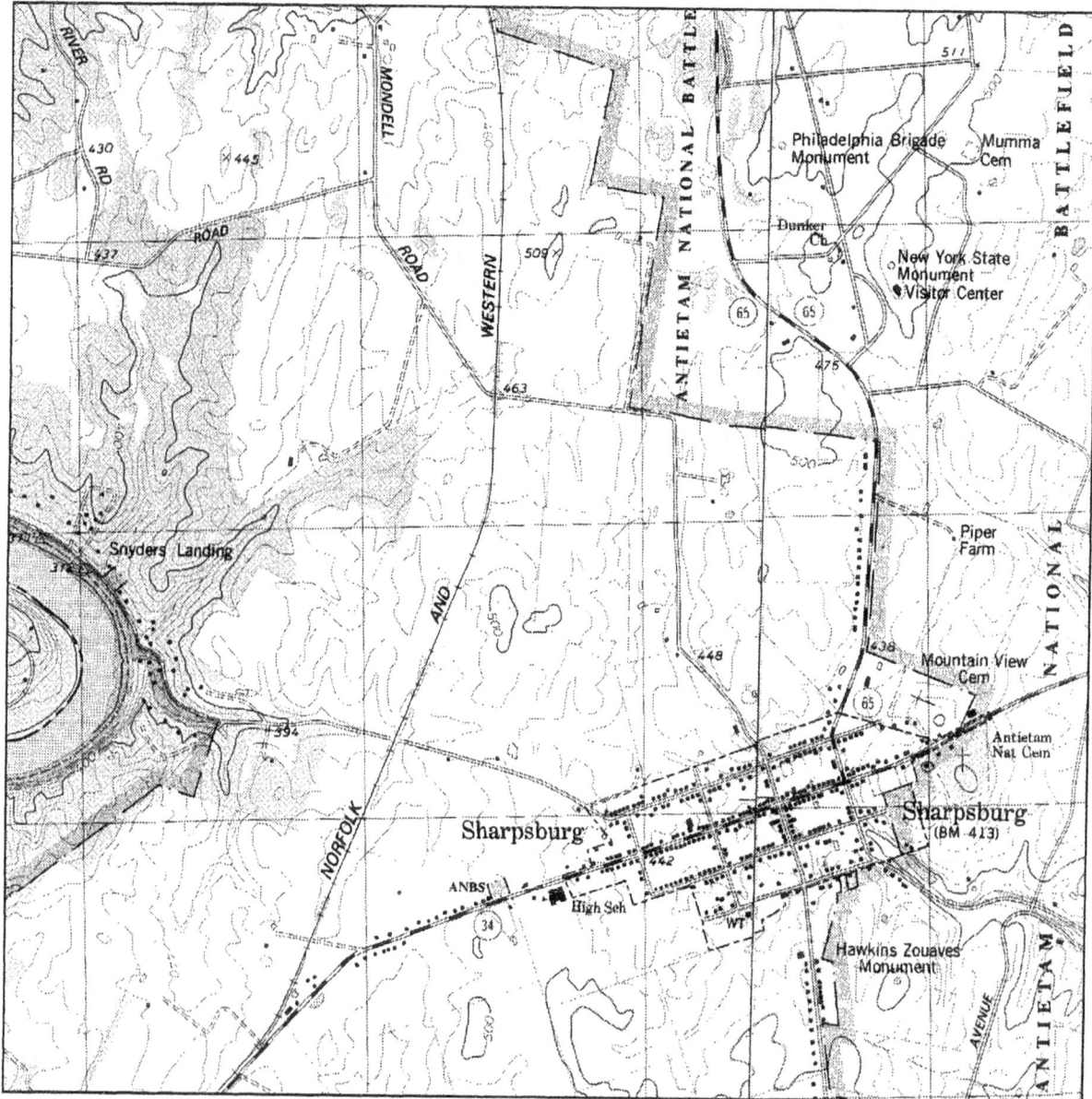

Here is a portion of the U.S.G.S. 7.5-minute Quadrangle ("topo") for "Shepherdstown, WV/MD." As discussed in Chapter 2, such maps are very valuable to the researcher, are available for much of the U.S., and are quite inexpensive. Notice the incredible detail and clarity. This map also reveals the "Grove House" at the western edge of Sharpsburg. That house is discussed here, appears in the background of the Lincoln photo, and is an ancestral home of Mrs. Driskill, the co-author. What a thrill for her to have learned of this.

Plan your visit and interview with the relative well ahead of time, all the while remembering that old folks tire easily, especially when called upon to think out and answer a long series of questions. So start with an easy question, and plan only to ask about a few important matters during the first interview session. Importantly: when you find that the person has tired, be polite; take a break or arrange a meeting at another time.

Sensitive Areas of Discussion

Since time immemorial, our people have had various, yet usually quite steadfast and, to them, proper views as to what they perceived to be matters of morality, especially concerning such subjects as adultery, illegitimacy, and divorce. By reason of these differing views, during an interview you may encounter a quite firm reluctance to continue with some subject or topic under discussion. Good researchers do not press such matters; they search elsewhere.

As mentioned earlier, perhaps during an interview or in some other place you will uncover a *black sheep* or two. When you do, remember that they are just as much a part of your family as are the upstanding citizens, and oftentimes are much more interesting. Further, as a family historian your task is to uncover, set forth, and preserve information. Good researchers never, ever consider it their privilege to pass judgment upon the conduct or character of ancestors.

Commencing The Interview

As you start your interview with the relative, also start a family unit chart (or family group sheet) for that person and his or her spouse, if there is or was one. As mentioned before, also be prepared to commence a family unit chart for EVERY other marriage of which you learn in the course of that interview.

Ask the relative to bring out old photos and mementos, not because you want to use them at that moment, because you usually won't (you will not know many of the people in the photos till after the interview), but because they will serve as valuable reminders for the person being interviewed. Be sure to utilize such keepsakes throughout your conversation. Incidentally, when you near the end of the interview, look again at those mementos and make sure you have knowledge of each of them, and be sure to ask to borrow those of significance in order that copies may be made for your records.

Folks sometimes prefer not to loan keepsakes or old photos. When such is the case, simply offer to pay all expenses if the relative will take the photos to be copied or the mementos to be photographed. Most researchers also offer to pay for an additional copy of such for the relative to have as his or her own.

In the matter of your questioning, let us assume that the person being interviewed is your Aunt Jane, your mother's sister. Now, an interview is not an exchange of ideas, nor is it a debate. Let Aunt Jane do almost all of the talking. Listen carefully, and even if you believe that you already know the answers, ask the questions anyway. Until she tires, the more you ask the more you will jog her memory.

An example of a subject that some family members will not want to discuss with you: From the 1862 records of the Probate Court of Hancock County, Ohio; a sworn statement by a citizen that a woman was dangerous to herself and her family and was "insane." The good family historian makes no judgments about such conditions and reports what is found without comment.

Ask all questions in terms of the relationships of the ancestors to the person being interviewed. Never ask questions in terms of the relationship of that ancestor to you. As examples, ask Aunt Jane "Who was your grandmother on your mother's side?"; not, "Who was my maternal great grandmother?" (Note that they would be the same person.) "Did your grandmother live here in this county?" Not, "Where did my great grandmother live?"

So, remember to always inquire on the basis of the kinship of an ancestor to the person being questioned. After all, since you already know the relationship of Aunt Jane to you, so after the interview you will be able to figure out how you tie in to the ancestor of whom you learned from Aunt Jane.

Some—perhaps, indeed, the most important—clues to the records of the lives of ancestors are gained by the simple question, "Where did they live?" Often the answer is unknown to the relative being questioned, however by continuing to inquire as to past places of residence of other relatives—their brothers, sisters, cousins, etc.—you may well uncover the home place of the ancestor you seek. So, if Aunt Jane does not know where her grandfather lived, ask, "Do you remember any of your grandfather's brothers or sisters—your parent's aunts and uncles?" If she does recall her mother's old Uncle Bill, then ask, "Where did Uncle Bill live?" Her answer may be of value later, and it may also have been the same place where the missing parents lived. It is most critical to remember that if the recollections of the person being interviewed differ from your other notes, so be it! As mentioned, you are not there to argue, and often you will find that you are the one who is very wrong.

Techniques For Jogging the Memory

People often will provide you with answers that they did not think they knew. Example: if you simply ask Aunt Jane when her grandfather died, as often as not she will say that she does not remember. Pursue the subject by asking if she had been born when he died or how old she was at the time of that death. Knowing that, you can simply add or subtract that many years to or from her birth date and you have his approximate death year. Or you might ask if she and her husband were married when that grandfather died. If the answer is yes, then ask if any of her children had yet been born at the date of the death. The answer may be "Why yes, John was just a baby then; we took him to the funeral. We drove, and it was so cold that day." By learning the birth date of the child, John, you then will again know approximately when the ancestor died, and also that it was in the winter. All that, even though Aunt Jane had said that she did not remember. (You also know that they had a family car.) Likewise, if she were to say "No, Jim was our middle child and wasn't born yet," thereby you will know that her grandfather died BETWEEN the birth year of her eldest child and the birth of Jim.

Just as women quite surely remember approximately how old a child was when this or that event occurred, men who lived in the 1930s, 1940s and 1950s often recall what make and model of automobile they had at the time of important events; cars were much, much more important and significant in earlier days than now, and there were not nearly so many brands and names. Indeed, many present-day older men are able to recite a list of all the vehicles they have owned, and even the color of each. So, when told by an older man that he can not recall when an event took place, ask what make of car he then had or drove; it may well refresh his memory. When other memories of dates fail, you might ask where the person being interviewed lived when the event occurred, then follow that question with an inquiry as to when they moved to or from that place. Quite usually a range of years will be gained thereby.

In years past, usually unlike now, automobiles were much more significant in the lives of their owners. Here, a 1927 registration was kept because, as did many men in those times, the owner constructed the vehicle from parts and was very proud of his work.

Finally, wars were (and are) long remembered and most important in the lives of all of us. The simple question, "Were any members of your family in a war?" often brings out many details not otherwise called to mind. If a date is not remembered, ask the person being interviewed if an event took place before the war, or, before or after World War II or the Korean or Vietnam War. In summary, always relate your questions to dates, events, or residences that are or were then probably important in the life of the person being interviewed.

Quite often, it is difficult for the person being interviewed to understand the precise nature of your interests. As an example, note that some certain second cousin of Aunt Jane with whom she played as a child may be well remembered and most important to her memory, however the same cousin may be quite remote from your inquiry and of little interest to your present research. So, unless you already have developed an interest in the families of aunts, uncles, and cousins (which are known as *collateral branches* or *collateral lines*), it is important that you direct your questions only towards those branches of the family through which you are related to the person being interviewed, and in which you have particular interests. But, remember that brief notes should be kept of comments concerning those collateral lines, since in the future such knowledge may help you untangle family lines in which you have a greater interest.

Keeping Control Of The Interview

Even though a conversation may move toward collateral lines in which you have little present interest, it is important to occasionally let the person being interviewed ramble. In so doing, they will relax just a bit and often will reveal facts about which you would not have thought to ask. Nevertheless, keep control of the interview, lest they stray too far from the purposes of your visit.

Additional Questions

In addition to asking where an ancestor and his family lived (especially if the interviewed person does not remember the answer to that question), try always to learn where the person being interviewed went when visiting elderly relatives, especially many years ago. Thereby, once again, new sources of records for future research will be revealed. Always ask the question, "Who is the oldest person you knew as a child?" In most families, there is someone who lived to be ninety (*nonagenarian*) or one hundred years old (*centenarian*), and through the *obituary* of that person you may learn many facts long forgotten by those now living.

Always note the date of the interview on the family unit chart. Knowing when you learned a new fact often will help later in evaluating conflicting information.

Always ask the person being interviewed if you may examine and study the notes in their family Bible, and then search through and copy all such notes precisely and thoroughly. Copy word-for-word even what you consider to be errors in spelling or mistaken dates. Remember, you very well may be the one who is wrong; we all have been.

Never fail to ask if there are any old letters, deeds, papers, or documents that you might read and copy (or keep). While there, be sure to take a photo of that relative, and have him or her hold a significant family heirloom. As soon as you can, preferably right then, and always, date the photographs.

Always seek to learn of family reunions that took place many years before. If there were any such events, seek diligently to learn when and where they were held in order that newspapers telling of the event later may be hunted down.

A fine photo showing an ancestor standing beside the first passenger train to leave Lansing, Michigan. A wonderful keepsake for that family, and a real prize for the researcher.

Always ask if any ancestors are known to have used any words of a foreign language. If any did so, you then may have a clue as to when that branch of the family first came to this country and from where. Even though most families continued to speak the language of the old country for only one generation after arriving here, since the English language often had no words that could be substituted for items such as favorite food (bratwurst, baklava), expressions of anger and profanity and other words not meant for the ears of children, old country words and expressions continued in use, often for several generations. Most of us long remember unusual expressions spoken by someone near to us, especially if spoken in a language other than English.

Then too, through foreign words—even those in a favorite recipe—one may gain a clue as to an area of prior residence. Even if they have no German lineage, few are the older women who do not have a recipe for a Pennsylvania Dutch dish if their grandmother or other close relative came from that area. Similarly, a family having a liking for grits or meat and biscuits for breakfast probably was influenced by persons from the South, and a taste for maple syrup probably came down from those of the northern states. So, even though pride in becoming American citizens led most folks to insist that their children learn and speak the language, a region or country of origin may arise from the speech of their descendants. But, remember that some nationalities, especially the northern Europeans, Greeks, and the Germans, clung stubbornly to both their past customs and their native language, oftentimes even for several generations.

Veterans

Always ask, especially, if there are stories or tales concerning wars in which members of the family fought or were otherwise involved. As with family traditions, war stories often carry down through a family for several generations. Why search out military records? Two good reasons: 1) You probably will be very proud of that ancestral military service, and 2) the records of veterans and their widows and children provide much information not to be found anywhere else.

A few words about war are important to your understanding. In early times, especially before the Civil War, there seldom was a *draft*—a conscription—as we know it. Most men enlisted only when the war came to the neighborhood or when they otherwise perceived that their families were in danger, and they were discharged in a very informal fashion when the fighting moved off to some other place. So it was that men generally voluntarily joined organizations or units being formed close to where they lived. Accordingly, if you learn of a Revolutionary or War of 1812 ancestor who joined the army at Reading, Pennsylvania, you have an excellent bit of evidence as to his approximate place of residence at the time of that enlistment. The likelihood that a veteran lived close to his place of enlistment or conscription exists even now; we still usually go to the local post office to enlist and are drafted from the area of our homes.

Be sure to ask where the person being interviewed believes a certain veteran to have lived; he or she may know, and thereby save you the effort of a search. At least try to learn of the area or region from which that ancestor is thought to have come, and, especially in the case of the Civil War, ask for what side he or she served or fought.

One old Tennessee mountain man related that his grandfather (whose name he did not recall) had been "...marched off by them soldiers and never heard of again." When asked in what war that incident took place, he replied, "Back there when the Democrats fought the Republicans." He was referring to the Civil War, of course. Having later learned of the whereabouts of the home of that grandfather at the time of the war, it was possible for the researcher to learn his name, what Confederate unit had taken him away, and even to where.

The National Archives and Records of Veterans

The available records vary from war to war, and to a considerable extent (even for the early wars) such records are still in existence, copies of which may be procured through the *National Archives* (see also Appendix 2). Write to the General Reference Branch (NNRG-P), National Archives and Records Administration, 7th and Pennsylvania Avenues, Washington, D.C., 20408, and request six or so sets of their forms required for such records (presently *Form NATF-80*) which are free of charge. You must use the prescribed forms to obtain copies of the records of veterans, since simple letters of request and inquiry are not acceptable at the Archives. The National Archives website address is **www.nara.gov**. Click on "How to Obtain Copies of NARA Records." You can request forms by e-mail from **inquire@nara.gov**.

For the wars up to and including the Indian wars of the late nineteenth century three categories of records usually were retained. They are a) those that have to do with the military movements and activities of the veteran, b) those that pertained to his *pension application* and the terms of the pension itself (whether or not he ultimately received one), and c) those which had to do with service connected *land grants*, i.e., the so-called *bounty land records*, again, whether or not it was ultimately determined that he really had any such rights.

So, if you want all categories searched (and you surely do), complete the forms for each category you want searched as fully as possible for each veteran, and then return the forms to the address designated in the forms. If you also desire the records of widow's pensions and benefits, forms must be submitted for them too. Unlike for veterans, for widows you will need only ask for the pension records since almost always in the early days they performed no military service.

The forms are easy to fill out. Note, though, the folks who do such searching are very busy, hence it is wise to order blank forms now (either through the Internet, by phone or by mail) in order that you may have some on hand when you need these in the future. Upon receipt of your completed forms, the folks there will do the records search for that ancestor, and if he or she is found in any of the categories mentioned, you will be notified that the records have been located. Thereupon, you will have a specified time within which to forward the fees designated for copies of those records. The amount of such fees will vary depending upon the number of entries or pages in that veteran's or widow's file. When sending in the forms, be sure to state that you want copies of ALL papers in the file, otherwise sometimes the clerks will select what they think appropriate and important, and you may not be sent all the available information.

Concerning the bounty land records, note that commencing in colonial times, and especially after the American Revolution and continuing through the Indian wars, nearly until the twentieth century, rights to quantities of land usually were granted as one of the several rewards for military service. Thereby, as with other inexpensive land settlement programs, the veterans were encouraged to take their families and clear and settle portions of the vast wilderness that yet remained. In fact, grants of land to veterans continued through the nineteenth century (1800s), and "homesteading" sponsored by both the States of the Union and the Federal government took place in Alaska down through the 1970s. Homesteading was even attempted by the State of Minnesota as recently as 1988, albeit unsuccessfully. All such governmental efforts to encourage settlement resulted in records and record keeping that will have great value to you.

In addition, throughout nearly all of our history, pensions or other benefits have been granted to those who served the nation in times of conflict. Then, after the deaths of those veterans, certain of those benefits also were granted to their survivors, especially their widows. The claims for all such benefits resulted in records valuable to the family historian. Notice too, the volunteer projects mentioned earlier having to do with cemeteries that appear on the Internet also have lists of known soldiers of most of our wars. Quite often such information is found on the web pages of states and may reveal at what place that person was enlisted or conscripted ("drafted").

Since, as mentioned, the methods used for recruiting and discharging our early volunteer veterans often were very informal, sometimes little or no record was kept by the government of the wartime activities of individual soldiers or even of their military units. Accordingly, later it often was impossible from the records alone to determine who should receive pensions, land, and other benefits, and who should not. So it was that after being placed under oath, the veterans (and their dependents or widows) who sought such rewards were required to give complete statements of those facts which rendered them eligible. In these sworn statements quite often were listed the parents of the veterans; their birthplaces and ages; their residencies before, during, and after the wars; marital status and the names of their wives; the names of dependents, brothers, and sisters; as well as the units in which they served, the battles in which they participated, and other wartime activities. Such records are often genealogical gold mines.

Concerning veterans' records, it is very important to remember that, generally speaking, until the year 1818, only those Revolutionary veterans who were maimed and disabled were awarded pensions. Then from 1818 until 1828, in order to qualify for a pension, a veteran had to demonstrate very reduced means—poverty, in fact. The poverty requirement resulted in affidavits and lists setting forth the total belongings owned by the veteran, which lists are delights to read. Then, after 1828 all of the still surviving veterans were pensioned. Finally, in 1836 widows of veterans also were granted monthly pensions.

Notice then, because of the changing requirements many men who served in the Revolution received no pensions whatever, and so often escape detection by the researcher. Why? Because if a Revolutionary veteran died BEFORE 1818 and was NOT maimed or disabled during service, or if he died BETWEEN 1818 and 1828 (between thirty-five and forty-five years after the end of the war) and was neither poverty stricken nor maimed, his name will not appear in the pension records, even though his widow might later appear.

So, where then will he be revealed? He likely will be found within the bounty land records, since his rights to land grants or to receive warrants that could be traded for land or sold, as the veteran chose, were not dependent upon his age, physical infirmity, or financial condition. So it is that the land warrant records may be the only evidence of his service that the researcher will find in the National Archives.

A word as to bounty land warrants and grants: in the early days (as now) the Federal government owned vast quantities of raw and undeveloped land. The warrants—vouchers of sorts, legal documents—awarded to veterans, others who had served the nation, and often ordinary citizens and politicians as well, could be exchanged for land at the "land offices" established for each area, territory, or group of territories. (As we shall see, the states also frequently owned land and made grants to their veterans in like fashion.) Each warrant related the quantity of land to which that person was entitled, depending upon the established value of his or her rank or services.

Then, generally speaking, even though there were many variations, upon arrival at the land office the veteran shopped through the list of available tracts of that quantity, selected the tract he wanted, had it surveyed (if necessary), and then, upon return of the survey showing no encroachment upon the lands of others, received the *grant*—the original deed—to that tract. That grant was written on very fine paper or *vellum* (calf, lamb, or kid skin) and while usually issued by the land offices and bearing their seals, sometimes were signed by the President who caused the *Great Seal Of The United States* to be affixed. The grant then was recorded in the courthouse of the territory or state where the land was situated, copies of many of which, as we shall see, may still be procured.

A copy of a very desirable document now in the Connecticut Archives: A copy of an order by Revolutionary War General Silliman that Isaac Sherwood be compensated for his service to the cause by traveling 90 miles on a horse. It was gained by submitting one of the forms required by that state.

Caution: since, as we have seen, land warrants owned by a veteran had value and legally could be sold by him, these often were. Further, such warrants sometimes were converted into land, whereupon the land itself was sold. So, land warrants, or the unsettled land resulting from such warrants, may never have provided a residence for a veteran ancestor. Indeed, he may never even have seen the property. Accordingly, you must not presume that an ancestor lived on a tract simply because he had a warrant for it, or because he once owned it.

Remember, though, that many a soldier was granted wilderness land, cleared it, built a house, raised a family, lived out his life, and found his final resting place there. So, be very careful in making assumptions based on land warrants found in the names of your ancestors.

In summary, unless you know when a veteran died and have knowledge of his physical condition and economic status, it is well to seek out all forms of records mentioned—land warrants and the pension and military activities files. Remember, any veteran not maimed, who also was not poverty stricken, and who did not live to extreme age, likely died without ever appearing in the pension records. But also remember that if his widow was alive after 1836, she may appear in those very records even though he did not, and her pension application and file will be every bit as complete as his would have been. Indeed, from the standpoint of genealogical information to be gained, widows' records often are more informative than are those of the veteran, since a widow's claim almost always rested entirely upon kinship to the veteran and not upon her military service, and so required proof of marriage, sworn statements concerning residences, children, etc.

Veterans' Records in Libraries and Archives

It also is important to note that during and after wars, particularly the Revolution and the War of 1812, the States of the Union and the U.S. Government quite usually permitted citizens to file claims for property destroyed by acts of war and for non-military services rendered or supplies furnished by them to the armed forces. Thereby will be revealed the locations or residences of ancestors, thus leading the researcher to the libraries and courthouses of that area. The many such claims have been the subject of many articles and books which can be found in nearly all large libraries and the archives of states.

You also must remember that not all existing veterans' records are housed in the National Archives. Especially in the early wars, many was the soldier who served in combat with a unit of a state militia or home guard, rather than in any national military unit. Such militia records very often were retained only in archives of states. Then too, as suggested above, many states had undeveloped land to grant as rewards for services. Accordingly, if you do not find an ancestor in the national records, yet by reason of his having been of military age you suspect that he did serve, you must search the records of those states and colonies which either existed or were carved out of those that did exist at the time of the war being researched.

From the National Archives; a copy of the certificate for the "Widow's Pension" of Mrs. Martha Midlam, the widow of Joseph Midlam who served in the War of 1812. Notice that his regiment is mentioned, making it possible for the researcher to learn of his wartime movements and actions.

I CERTIFY, That the within named *Silas J Drake*
a *private* of Captain *C. Tacitus Allen* Company (*7*) of the
Second Regiment of *Va H Arty*, born in *Mecklenburg*
in the State of *Virginia*, aged *31* years, *6* feet *1*
inches high, *dark* complexion, *dark* eyes, *dark* hair, and by
occupation a *farmer* was enlisted by *Capt Allen*
in *Lunenburg* on the *25* day of *January* 186 *2*
to serve *war* years, and is now entitled to discharge by reason of
Ascitis
   The said *Silas J Drake* was last paid by *Capt Allen*
to include the *31st* day of *October* 186 *2*, and has pay
due from that date to the present date.
   There is due to him _____ Dollars traveling allowance
from _____, the place of discharge, to _____ the
place of enrolment, transportation not being furnished in kind.
   There is due him _____
   He is indebted to the Confederate States _____ Dollars
on account of _____
   Given in duplicate at _____, this _____ day of _____ 186 .

                          O Tacitus Allen
                          Captain Commanding Company.

For pay from *31* of *Oct* 186 *2*, to *16* of
December 186 *2*, being *1* months and *15* days,
at *eleven* Dollars per month,   - - -   *16* | *50*
For pay for traveling from _____ to
_____, being _____ miles, at
ten cents per mile, - - - - - - - -

                          Amount, - -
Deduct for clothing overdrawn, _____

                          Balance paid, - - *$16* | *50*

RECEIVED of *Maj Jno Aguble* C. S. Army, this *18*
day of *Dec* 186*2*, *Sixteen* Dollars and *50*
Cents, in full of the above account.

(Signed duplicates.)   *Silas J Drake*

WITNESS: _____

*A copy of a precious document for a descendant: Here is the Surgeon's Certificate releasing from
duty Confederate artilleryman, Silas J. Drake of Virginia. It is said here that he had "ascitis;" that
ailment also called "dropsy of the abdomen" (a collection of fluid in the abdominal cavity). Notice
that it also reveals his height, weight, eye and hair color, and states that he was a "farmer." It
was obtained by a request to the National Archives in Washington, D.C.*

When searching for Revolutionary ancestors and their families, keep in mind that most large libraries have very fine indexes to the records of the *Society of Daughters of the American Revolution (D.A.R.)*, which contain thousands of names of patriot veterans, as well as the names of myriad descendants who, by reason of the service of their ancestors, are now or were once affiliated with that organization or sought to be so associated. The magnificent library of the D.A.R. is in Washington, D.C., and is open to the public. So too is the fine library of the *Society of Sons of the American Revolution (S.A.R.)* located in Louisville, Kentucky. Again though, remember that those records do not contain the names of every single veteran.

It also is important to remember that the states and border states which comprised or adjoined the Confederate States of America have many, if not most, of the records of those who served the South during the Civil War. So, as with searching for those who served in the state militias of the earlier times, you must seek records from the state archives for those who served the Confederacy. As before, write the archives in the capitols of the states where the soldier lived at or about the time of that war (1861-1865) and ask what requirements they may have for gaining copies of such records.

If you find that an ancestor was a veteran of any of our wars, you are eligible to be considered for membership in some of the organizations that arose from such service. Among the many such organizations, the D.A.R., the S.A.R., and the *S.R. (Sons of the Revolution)* have to do with the Revolution; the *General Society of the War of 1812* and the *Ladies of 1812*, serve those who have ancestors involved in that cause; the *S.C.V.* and the *U.D.C. (Sons of Confederate Veterans* and *United Daughters of the Confederacy)* are concerned with the Old South; the *S.U.V.* and *D.U.V. (Sons of Union Veterans* and *Daughters of Union Veterans)* are made up of descendants of those who served the North; and, of course, the *American Legion*, the *V.F.W. (Veterans of Foreign Wars)* and the *D.A.V. (Disabled American Veterans)* serve the wars of the twentieth century. As said, there are many, many other organizations for which you may be eligible as a result of the military service of an ancestor. Your library will have lists of patriotic organizations, any one of which will be glad to hear from you.

Societies and Clubs

Speaking of societies, since the earliest times, and in this country—especially since the middle of the nineteenth century (1800s)—men and women have sought to be members of societies (patriotic and otherwise), clubs, organizations, sororities, and fraternities. Thus, it is quite likely that one or more of your ancestors will be found to have so belonged. *The Order Of The Cincinnati, United Daughters of the Confederacy, Sons of Confederate Veterans, Rebekah Lodge, Daughters of 1812, Sons of Union Veterans, Sons Of The Revolution (to be distinguished from the S.A.R.), Colonial Dames, the Eastern Star, Masons, Shrine, Order of Red Men, Woodmen of the World, Odd Fellows, Moose,* and the *Elks* are but a few of the very many. By contacting the local secretary of those organizations (try the telephone directory or a search of the Internet), or by inquiring at the state archives concerning now defunct societies, you may uncover records of memberships, which often reveal ages, dependents, marriage dates, and other interesting and important facts nowhere else to be found.

Churches

What of churches and religious affiliations? They are extremely valuable sources of information! In the early days, virtually everyone went to church. They did so a) because they very often were God-fearing, b) because the law often required it, and c) by reason of the pleasure and social value of such meetings and gatherings. So be sure to ask about church affiliations of all ancestors mentioned or discussed. Draw the locations of such churches on your map, and whether or not those churches are still in existence, drive out there, take pictures, and inquire of the pastors or other church officers as to the whereabouts of the birth, baptism, death, and other records of their congregation.

If the church you seek is yet active and in another city or town, you can usually find the mailing address on the Internet. Once that is in hand, you can write letters requesting information about that ancestor or congregation. Then too, if you learned from Aunt Jane that she thought the godparents of a relative lived in a certain city, you can also find an address for those persons through the Internet.

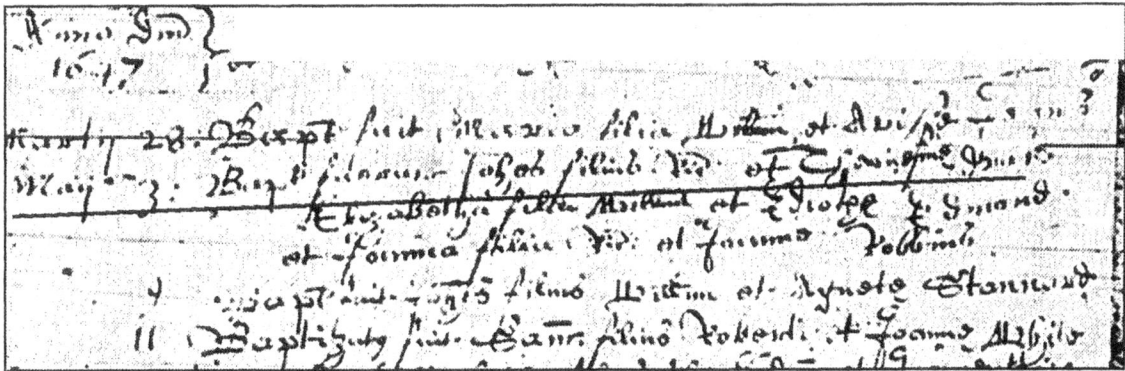

A wonderful discovery for the researcher: Here is a baptismal record written in Latin and copied from the original records of the "Church of St. Peter and St. Paul" in South Petherton, Somerset, England. Dated May 3, 1647, it reveals that baptised that day was "John, son of Richard and Thomaseine Drake." Notice that John was spelled "Johan."

Records of such events as baptisms, deaths, confirmations, and even the meetings of early members often are still in existence, and often such sources are quite complete and incredibly helpful. So, if available to you, search such records very carefully. During that search, it is important to remember that nearly always the folks who were named as witnesses, sponsors, and participants in baptisms, christenings, confirmations, and dedications of children were relatives of the child—parents, aunts, uncles, grandparents, etc. Likewise, godparents usually were relatives. Remember that even if they were only friends, all such sponsors and participants had some relationship to the family, so their presence provides clues for the careful researcher.

Note also that because there often were many children born to a family, christenings and baptisms were commonplace, and therefore the sponsors and witnesses at such events quite usually resided not far away. By reason of the time consumed and the difficulties of moving about on foot or by horse, folks normally did not travel long distances for such commonplace events. Thus, the neighborhood or area in which an ancestor lived may be revealed by who was present at church events, common occurrences, and family gatherings.

If the old family church is no longer active, then visit a nearby church of the same denomination, and there ask about to the location of the records (or even of the last record keeper) of the inactive old congregation. When the records are not to be found locally, note carefully the name of and approximate year that the activities in the old church ended; you can use that information upon your next visit to the state capitol. Then, when at the state capitol and archives (of which later), inquire as to the location of any regional repository for that religious denomination. Two examples: in Nashville, Tennessee, you will find a substantial collection of materials and records pertaining to many early Baptist congregations, and the American Jewish Archives are located in Cincinnati, Ohio.

Likewise, and simply for the asking, there are available to us many other collections of church records. Nearly always these archives are open to the public and are free. Incidentally, in the early days the best records were kept by the Quakers, Catholics and the Lutherans, to which list, after about 1840, one must add the Mormons. Remember too that Orders of Sisters (nuns) often owned and operated schools, and their valuable records of students sometimes may be uncovered simply by inquiring of the local parish priest.

Cemeteries

Finally, and very importantly, many churches maintained cemeteries, the records for which are often kept locally with the other church documents. So, inquire of the pastors, clerks, or members of the congregation concerning such facilities and records.

Always ask Aunt Jane for the names and locations of ALL other cemeteries wherein family members are thought to be buried, and carefully locate them on your map. Much will be learned by your visits there. Note too that most cemeteries—even the smallest ones—have formal or informal names, e.g., "Bishop Cemetery," "Pleasant Hill Cemetery," etc. Make a note on the family unit chart of any such names for use in your later inquiries in that area or in cemetery lists.

Since walking horses and mourning people moved at only about three miles an hour, ancestors nearly always were buried within three or four miles of their homes, and, just as now, very few persons were buried off by themselves. So, the locations of graves usually indicate that the dead lived nearby, and graves which are located close to those of your ancestors very well may be those of relatives. Note all information found on every family grave marker, and make notes of the dates and names found on the headstones immediately surrounding those graves. As suggested above, if the cemetery once was a churchyard inquire of folks living nearby as to the name and denomination of that old church, that information to be used later when visiting the church record repositories or the archives.

Remember that most headstones deteriorate in a few score years, and within your lifetime grave markers that are now difficult to read will be illegible and lost forever. So, take photos of all family headstones and carefully preserve a record of what is written on each. If the carving in the stone is difficult to read, often the problem may be solved by brushing away the dirt and debris with a soft bristle brush (not metal), then placing thin brown wrapping or meat paper tightly over the stone, and thoroughly rubbing red or blue carpenters' chalk (available in every hardware store) or dark crayons over the paper.

Another easy way is to spray the stone with ordinary shaving cream, and then quickly wipe over it with a squeegee such as is used to clean windows. For a few seconds the old writing often will be quite visible.

In early times, particularly in the tidewater counties of the colonies from Maryland south, there was no native stone from which to make cemetery markers, and only the wealthy or nearly so had the means to have such stone shipped from the other colonies. For those reasons, many of your southern ancestors were buried without markers other than those made of wood which are now long turned to dust. Then too, even in those settled areas where stone was available merely for the taking, stone carvers either had not yet arrived or charged unaffordable fees for their services. So it was that very often the men of the family made monuments to the dead with a piece of ordinary fieldstone and a "cold chisel," often inscribing only the initials. Nevertheless, even these sometimes become readable through the use of chalk or shaving cream.

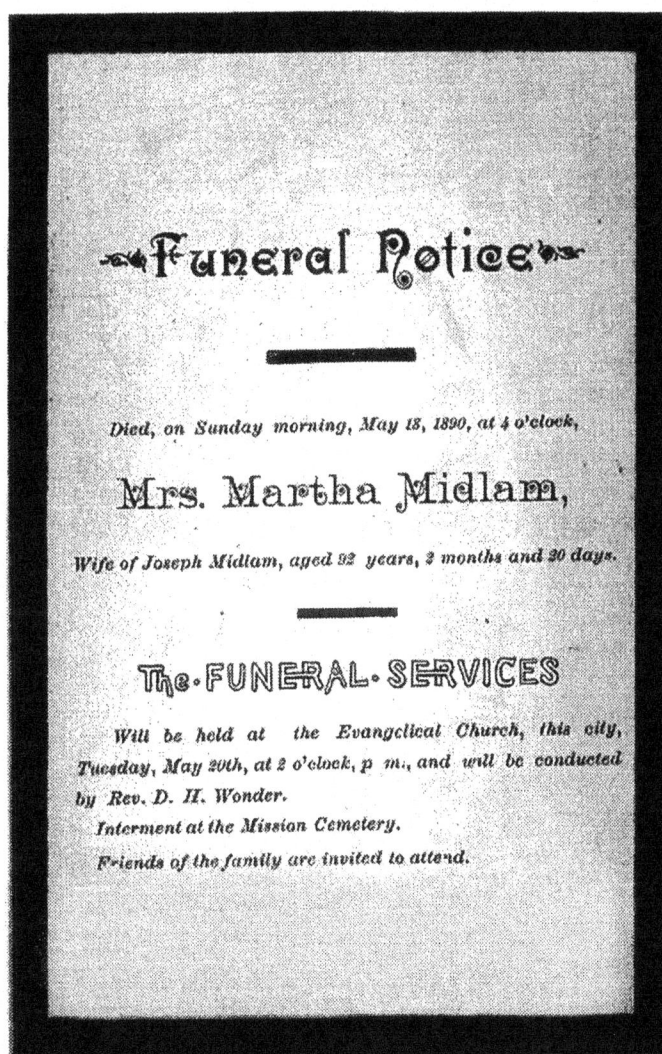

Though the monuments may have deteriorated beyond recognition, some families have preserved "mourning cards" from many years past. Here is one for Mrs. Martha Freeburn Midlam, dated May 18, 1890. Notice that it also names her deceased husband, Joseph Midlam, and gives her age at death as 92 years, 2 months, and 20 days; born Feb. 28, 1798.

If the cemetery has an office and record keeper (called a *sexton*), ask if you may search the *Index to Interments*. Check it for all persons who had the surnames you are searching. Do so, even if you think they are not related. If there is no cemetery office, ask a neighbor for the name of the caretaker, grounds keeper, or person who mows the grass, and then inquire of him or her. Such folks often know many very important details concerning families buried there and of others like you who have visited and inquired after specific families and names. Mowing a cemetery time after time lends a considerable depth of knowledge, hence such folks often will know quite positively if a family name is not familiar to them, thus saving you much time and also revealing that you probably are in the wrong place.

As mentioned, be sure to ask the caretaker if others have inquired after the same graves or surnames. If they have, you may establish a most valuable research friend, relative, or family line. Some cemeteries even have logbooks or journals in which researchers record their names, addresses, and the names of the deceased for whom they are searching. You should sign it too.

Notice too that there are many volunteer projects on the Internet that list cemeteries and the persons buried there. Searching under the name of the county or state will often give you that much needed information. Once you have it, you can write to the volunteer group doing that project, and there learn much.

Back to the interview and the family traditions and favorite stories. Remember that while the details of such stories are often quite unreliable, such tales almost invariably contain elements and a core of truth, which facts will provide very valuable clues for future research. So, ask questions about traditions and stories and, as always, make complete notes, even if those tales are fanciful or hardly believable.

After you have completed the interviews, obtained the veterans' records, visited the churches and cemeteries, and assembled, recorded, and organized the information obtained from those sources, you are ready to consider the Internet.

3

The Internet

In the first two chapters you have read the word, *research*, describing your activities in searching for your family history. We have spoken of the many tools you may use to find your ancestors. The Internet also is a research tool, and a very valuable one. Many resources will be at your disposal with this tool.

There are: maps, churches, cemeteries, the National Archives and veterans' records, to name a few. In later chapters you will find so many "tools" that you might commence a separate notebook just to list the resources at your disposal. Any time you become discouraged, bring out your notebook and review your many options.

The Internet, with all its mystique, is still only a research tool. You may have been in line at the market or having lunch with friends when someone told about the wonderful information they had found on the Internet. The word Internet may or may not be foreign to you, but it is only one of the many resources you may use, so don't let anyone convince you that all your answers will be found there. You will find a great deal of information, but it is still only one of several sources.

Let's proceed with the assumption that you have a computer and a connection by way of a service provider to the Internet and the World Wide Web (WWW). Is there information that might assist you in the search for YOUR family history? Yes indeed! And, each and every day, more and more information is added to the Internet. It is not and never will be the "end all" and "be all" for your research, but it may provide you with very important information.

The convenience of this wonderful medium also is a plus for those of us with small children or an ill relative that might require us to be at home many hours of the day. Then too, those of us who work days and can only research after everyone in our family has gone to bed will enjoy searching at night when it is convenient for us and quiet.

What Can Be Found

So, we are connected to the Internet. Now what can we expect to find? More than you dreamed of, but less than you would like. In the next chapter we will discuss the library and all its wonders. Like there, by using one of the many search engines of the Internet, such as Yahoo! or Excite or Infoseek, if we type in the words "Library of Congress" and click Enter, we will be taken to the web page of that wonderful facility and we can read at our leisure of their vast holdings.

Most people believe, as we do, that genealogy information is meant to be shared. Consequently, many folks make web pages that list their ancestors and often the proof they have found for their relationships to these ancestors. Almost all web pages will have e-mail addresses, and you can write to them and ask questions, and often the two of you can share information.

After you have finished with the Library of Congress, try typing in your surname at the search engine, lets say, "Mulvaney." Each instance where the name Mulvaney is found will be brought forward for you to examine. Sometimes there may be few, and sometimes hundreds. One search will often lead you to another area for research. Since we also know that the name Mulvaney is Irish, we might search for archives and libraries in Ireland. You get the idea.

One of the most interesting and important areas of information we will seek, will be the state or region of the country where our folks once lived. Our people did not catch an airplane at London Heathrow and fly into Richmond International. Their arrival period, from where they came, and the region in which they settled will fill in many of the questions of why they came. Did they have friends or relatives who had already settled there? Did the rolling hills of Virginia remind them of home? Did they believe they there would find others of their faith?

Just as the year 2000 brought fears of computer errors, the change from the Julian Calendar to the Gregorian Calendar brought concern to businesses of the period 1680-1753. Here, from New Hampshire, is a deed dated January 7th, "1741/1742." Though all knew that the change-over was coming, because until 1752 March was the first month of the year and March 25 was celebrated as the first day of each new year, those who wrote this deed hoped to avoid confusion by writing both years together.

Researching the areas of the country where our ancestors settled is fun and easy with the many Internet resources the search engines will find for us. We can seek and gain information from the earliest time periods, right up to and including present day material. Then too, the regional information that you may find on the Internet will save you many trips to the neighborhood library.

Volunteer Projects

There are also volunteer projects that gather public information from contributors who use the Internet and post that information for all to see. Volunteers, just like us (and you, one of these days), can share data we have gathered and place this information on the web page of that county and state. Since e-mail addresses are usually included, many fellow researchers may respond by writing to you, and before long you may have found a new "cousin."

Knowledge of the formation—the *genesis*—of counties will often tell you where to write for copies of documents and reports. For instance, your ancestor may have been born in one county and have never moved from that farm over a period of many years, even though the name of that county where his farm was and is yet located may have changed three times or more over those years! Volunteers from hundreds of counties have listed when their counties were formed and the parent counties from which such were carved, that information now available to you through the search engines.

Internet information may guide you to Civil War registers that will help you find your ancestor. There are lists of the many military units—regiments, battalions, divisions, corps, naval units—along with the names of men and women who served in these many units and battles. One of these lists may have the very ancestor you seek.

You can imagine our excitement when we searched one of the many county web pages and discovered a roster of a unit of Virginia Artillery, Confederate States Army, and there found our Great Grandfather, Silas James Drake. That roster revealed that he enlisted on January 25, 1862, at St. John's Church, Lunenburg County, Virginia, and that he was discharged at age 31, on December 16, 1862 by a Confederate army surgeon. The document continued; he was a farmer and had been born in Lunenburg County, Virginia. All this information from just one "hit" on the Internet! (See p. 21.)

Armed with this information, we wrote to the National Archives in Washington, D.C., to learn if they too had a record of the service of our Silas James Drake. Even though many documents concerning Confederate soldiers remain in the archives of the Southern States and not in the National Archives, we were fortunate; he was there. We filled out required form (at this writing, the NATF-80) and sent it in. (The address of the National Archives is set out for you in Appendix 2 and in the preceding Chapter.)

Books and their written words will always be an important part of your search. Sometimes the only place to find books concerning a certain state or county will be through publishers of genealogical information. These companies also publish family history books, so your particular surname may already have been the subject of a book written about the family. As an example, the book, *From Mill Wheel To Plowshare* is about our Revolutionary War ancestor, Major Christian Orndorff. In that single book we found much of our Orndorff lineage.

The publisher of this book is Heritage Books, Inc. Heritage has a web page that features a listing of all of their books and CDs, so—again from your computer chair—you may view what is available for purchase. Some of the books can actually be read online, by subscriing to the "Heritage Library." Many other publishers of books and CDs are to be found on the Internet, as well. Instead of waiting at your mailbox for catalogs, the net provides you with the opportunity to view the available inventories and make your selections from your computer.

In a later chapter we will discuss naturalization records. Our ancestors who came to America after the American Revolution quite usually were required to state the country or area from which they came and, of course, give their names. This was not limited to the names of men alone, but also was required of the women and the children.

One of the most exciting projects now underway is that directed by Mr. Lee Iacocca and the Immigration History Center at Ellis Island. Difficult as it is to believe, between 1892 and 1954 twelve million immigrants were admitted to this country through Ellis Island alone. Over 100 million of all LIVING Americans can trace their roots to ancestors who came through that processing center. When this project is completed, information as to these many millions of immigrants will be available for those on the Internet in order that we be able to search for our ancestors' names and see the country of origin of those hardy people. Without the Internet, you would have to travel to New York to see such exciting information.

This might be a good time to mention the passage of time and very old or ancient documents and memorabilia. These papers, books, and mementos that reveal so much about our dearly departed ancestors are still only made of paper and ink or other materials that require care. The handling of these mementos, especially old documents, by many indifferent individuals, even before they ever reached court houses or finally the archives, have left them in danger of disintegration. Computer technology will allow us to save these precious materials for all time.

In a later chapter we will discuss *Care of Records*, but for now we should mention the wonderful and safe method of preservation by digitizing documents. Many large libraries have the staff and knowledge to transfer and preserve, through computer generated images, copies of these old documents. We then can visit these libraries through the WWW and view many of these documents without ever leaving home. We also can print out such documents and write for certified copies, should we choose. With such a permanent record, these precious documents and writings will be there for another 300 years and perhaps much more.

Records of the States of the Union

Another exciting research tool found on the Internet was placed there, for all to use, by the Bureau of Land Management (BLM). This site (**www.blm.gov**) contains the official land patent records for selected Eastern States. The Bureau plans to add even more states in the future, so you might check back now and again to learn whether or not your state is listed, if it is not now. The states on-line at this writing—and fully searchable—are Alabama, Arkansas, Florida, Illinois, Indiana, Louisiana, Michigan, Minnesota, Mississippi, Missouri, Ohio and Wisconsin.

Some of us do not have good eyesight, and to read census records on microfilm at the library is a chore, even if you have perfect eyesight. Many of the volunteer projects that we mentioned earlier also have undertaken to place on the Internet as many of the United States Census Records as time has permitted.

If you were born in the twentieth century and are just beginning your family history research, you are the most fortunate of all, particularly because of present and rather recent laws now requiring the preservation of vital information! Census records are full of information, and many of the census records of the twentieth century are now on the Internet. As with their other efforts, the volunteers have transcribed the 1910 and 1920 Census records for your search.

Earlier birth records (eighteenth and nineteenth centuries) sometimes were recorded in the records of churches, including when and if a child was baptized or its birth recorded by a midwife. Marriages, births, and deaths now require licenses to be gained from and filed with the state where that event took place. Notice though, early marriages often were performed by ministers, preachers, and justices of the peace, the information then having been given to a town clerk or other magistrate the next time the officiating minister or official went to town. Many of the records of such churches and of the town clerks or magistrates are now on the Internet and searchable by the names of the churches, towns or counties.

What if you don't know your birth name or the names of your parents because you were adopted or *fostered out?* In the past, often you had very few options. Today, with the assistance of the Internet, you will find many sites with information to help and guide you. We found an Adoption Triad Outreach that does not perform searches for you, but does guide you by providing information and tools so that you may undertake your own search. That organization also has a free international adoption reunion registry that is available for you. Here you may enter your search information and read the registry of posts and inquiries made by other searchers.

Most of our early ancestors belonged to a religious group, order, sect, or congregation. The history of these early "churches" often may be found on the Internet and thereby guide you to the regions of the country where these religious groups settled. For instance, the early German Mennonites of our family settled in the Lancaster area of Pennsylvania. We later discovered that the land for the Groffdale Mennonite Church was donated by our ancestor, Hans Groff (GROVE). Searching the WWW, you often can locate these churches and write for information.

Latter-Day Saints

The Family History Department of The Church of Jesus Christ of Latter-Day Saints ("LDS"; "Mormons") is an international leader in genealogical research with some 3,200 Family History Centers located around the world. The Mormons now are placing some of their computerized records on the net. We feel the most important contribution will be the Family History Library Catalog, with a list of their holdings that you may view by visiting a Family History Center near you.

If microfilm of the record you desire is not available locally, the Centers will order such for you. All the Centers coordinate with the LDS Library in Salt Lake City, which has over two million rolls of microfilm containing copies of original records and documents from more than a hundred countries. These records include vital, census, church, land and probate records and many other types of materials of genealogical value. You surely will want to search this very valuable source. Hopefully, many of these records may become available for viewing on the Internet.

Historic Photographs

One final site we want to mention—and believe us, there are many WWW sites—is the U. S. Army Military History Institute (USAMHI) in Carlisle, Pennsylvania. This Department of the Army website (**http://carlisle-www.army.mil**) will allow you to search for photographs that were taken usually having to do with our wars and the people who served during those conflicts. Here you may search by battlefield, surname, photographer, name of military unit, or even by using a combination of terms. You may e-mail a request for specific photographs, and if they are available, copies of these will be sent to your address. You may then decide if you want to purchase a true photocopy of the machine copies you have examined.

The USAMHI also has histories of many, many military units—regiments, battalions, divisions, corps, etc.—that served in various conflicts, campaigns and wars. You may search this site for these units and there learn the locations, dates, and often many details of their encounters.

There are so many exciting places for you to search on the Internet, and we can only hope that you will explore this incredibly useful research tool. But, remember, as we said before, the Internet is only ONE of many tools that you can use in your search for your family history. Take advantage of all the tools, and soon the story of your ancestors will unfold before you.

4

Libraries

In large part, family research is a search of indexes, and libraries have plenty of these. Most of us do not have direct access to the giant libraries and renowned collections of genealogical materials, of which there are several. The *Library of the Church of Jesus Christ of Latter Day Saints* (*LDS* or *Mormon Library*) in Salt Lake City, Utah; the *Public Library of Allen County* in Fort Wayne, Indiana; and the collection in the *Library of the City of New York* perhaps are the best known and largest of the great American sources. Further, all state capitals and most large cities have substantial collections, especially concerning that state, the surrounding area, and many of those areas from which local peoples migrated. All are available for your careful use and usually are free. Smaller, nevertheless equally important to you, are the numerous collections dedicated to special groups such as German immigrants, Baptists, physicians, members of the armed forces, etc., and, of the utmost significance, those collections found in nearly every local library.

Commencing Your Library Research

To commence your library research, walk in and ask the librarian to direct you to the family history (genealogy) section and to the genealogy *catalog*. The genealogy catalog may be with the main catalog or may be by itself, and may be either in the old card form or, more probably now, computerized (or both). If the catalog is on computer, do not be intimidated. Read the instructions, and ask for help if you do not understand.

Always remember, however, that librarians are not there to do your research, nor do they have time to listen to long stories about your family, no matter how interesting such tales may seem to you. In short, while the library folks will be happy to help in many ways and to direct you to materials which are available for that county and area, you have to do the work; they will help you locate the books you need, but you have to do the reading.

Changing Boundaries

To do good library research, you must make some adjustments in your thinking. Today, the states of the Union are quite usually divided into well established cities, towns and counties, the last in turn divided into townships or districts, townships into precincts, etc. While we are accustomed to the unchanging nature of the boundaries of such *political subdivisions*, that was not always the way of things. As a result, one of the most common shortcomings of the newcomer to family research is the failure to realize that nearly every political division had its beginnings as a part of another one or more larger and different townships, counties, states, or territories. Note too that while their boundaries frequently change, cities and towns also may be divided into wards and precincts.

All of our present states and territories underwent such changes, and by noticing these, you will gain interesting and helpful insight into the history of our great nation. As an example: nearly all of what now is Ohio, Indiana, Illinois, Michigan, Wisconsin and Minnesota was a part of New France until the conclusion of the French and Indian War, after which those lands became English. They then became part of the Northwest Territory and soon after the American Revolution were governed largely by the Ordinance of 1787. Later—in 1803—the part of that territory now called Ohio was admitted to the Union as a state and was, then, divided into six counties, some reserved Indian lands, and a military district set off as a source of lands for veterans, etc. By 1820—its counties all the while being divided into townships, sections, etc.— Ohio had been further subdivided into sixty-two counties, and, finally, by 1860, as today, there were eighty-eight (88) counties, all divided into townships as their individual needs varied and demanded. (Note here also that what you know as counties and townships may elsewhere, now and in times past, be called precincts or manors or even towns.)

In addition to the changes themselves, the reasons for such changes are important to the researcher. Over a period of now some three centuries, as land was gained from France, Russia, Spain, and the Indians, our settlements have continually moved generally west and south. Indeed, such was the state of affairs until virtually all of the land between the oceans and between Canada and Mexico was settled and had become a part of our nation. Further, even as each new county and state was being established, pioneers seeking land already were moving outward and away from the newest settlements.

As people moved, so did their government. Just as before they migrated to the new settlements, the outermost of the settlers had to have continuing access:
   a) to those offices established for the preservation of documents and other evidence, particularly concerning land transactions and death (land grants, deeds, leases, mortgages, records of veterans, and wills and estates);
   b) to the law, which, it was hoped, would protect such rights and privileges (courts, judges, and law enforcement officers such as sheriffs, constables, and justices of the peace); and
   c) to a place positive from which taxes could be assessed and to which the same might be paid, the last mentioned surely more desired by the governing bodies and officials than by the settlers.

The place where those offices and facilities were located quite usually was (and is) called the *county seat*, so called since that was the seat of government; that place where officials literally sat and conducted the affairs of the public and common good.

In early times, much more so than now, the need to remain at home to tend to and protect their families, farms, and livelihoods, brought the belief and virtual requirement that not more than a single day of travel should be required to attend to government business. As a result, even though a distinct minority frequently traveled about for reasons of commerce and land activities, most of our farming pioneer ancestors were reluctant to leave home for any period of time. Thus, the more distant the county seats were from those farmers, the less accessible government was.

Since nearly all travel had to be on foot, on horseback, or in small boats, the distance between county seats ended up being not much more than about thirty miles (except in the great prairie states where the cattle grazing business required much larger boundaries). So it was that as soon as the outermost settlers were thirty, forty, or so miles distant, and the landholders and their lands were sufficient in voice, number, and tax dollar value to justify the formation of such, another county was formed. Each new county was given a name and almost always was assigned quite specific boundaries.

So, why are these historical facts and reasons important to the family researcher? Because, by reason of the continuing changes in county names and boundaries, a frontier farmer might settle, build a home, raise a family, never move, and yet over his lifetime be a resident of several different townships, counties, and even of different states of the Union. You must remain constantly conscious of that likelihood if you are to adequately research the lives of your ancestors.

Examples? There are many. Suppose you find that an ancestor and his family settled in Cumberland County, Pennsylvania, in 1770. Then you find that in 1776 they were no longer listed there yet when you happen to search the Bedford County tax lists you find them again. Thereafter, in 1787, they disappear from the Bedford records, however they then turn up in the records of Huntingdon County. They sure moved around a lot, didn't they? To the contrary, perhaps not at all. Perhaps not even once!

You see, part of old Cumberland County was carved away to form Bedford County in 1771, and following that (in 1787) Bedford provided the land from which was formed Huntingdon. Thus your people could have settled on land in Cumberland County after the Indian title was extinguished in 1760, lived and raised their families there over the following thirty years—as many did—and casually looked on and went about their business while their land became, first, a part of Bedford, and then, seventeen years later, a part of the new Huntingdon County.

Moreover, suppose that ancestor died on the home place and left it to a son who, with his family, continued to live there until his death in 1850. In 1846, Huntingdon too was carved into two parts; one remained Huntingdon, but the other part became the new Blair County. So, if your ancestral farm was in that part of the old Indian land which ultimately became Blair County, you would find the estate records of that son and his family in the Blair courthouse. Over a period of but ninety years the family would have lived in four distinct governmental entities and yet not have moved even once. Thus, as you move backward through the years, to keep track of just that single family you would be called upon to seek out the records in the courthouses for Blair, Huntingdon, Bedford and Cumberland counties.

Other examples are too numerous to mention, however notice that Bourbon County, of what is now Kentucky but once was Virginia, contributed a portion of its territory to more than fourteen of the presently existing Kentucky counties. Moreover, many early settlers of land which is now in Kentucky and Tennessee considered themselves to be and, in fact were, Virginians and North Carolinians, respectively. Portions of Westmoreland County, Pennsylvania, and all of what now is West Virginia were in Virginia at one time.

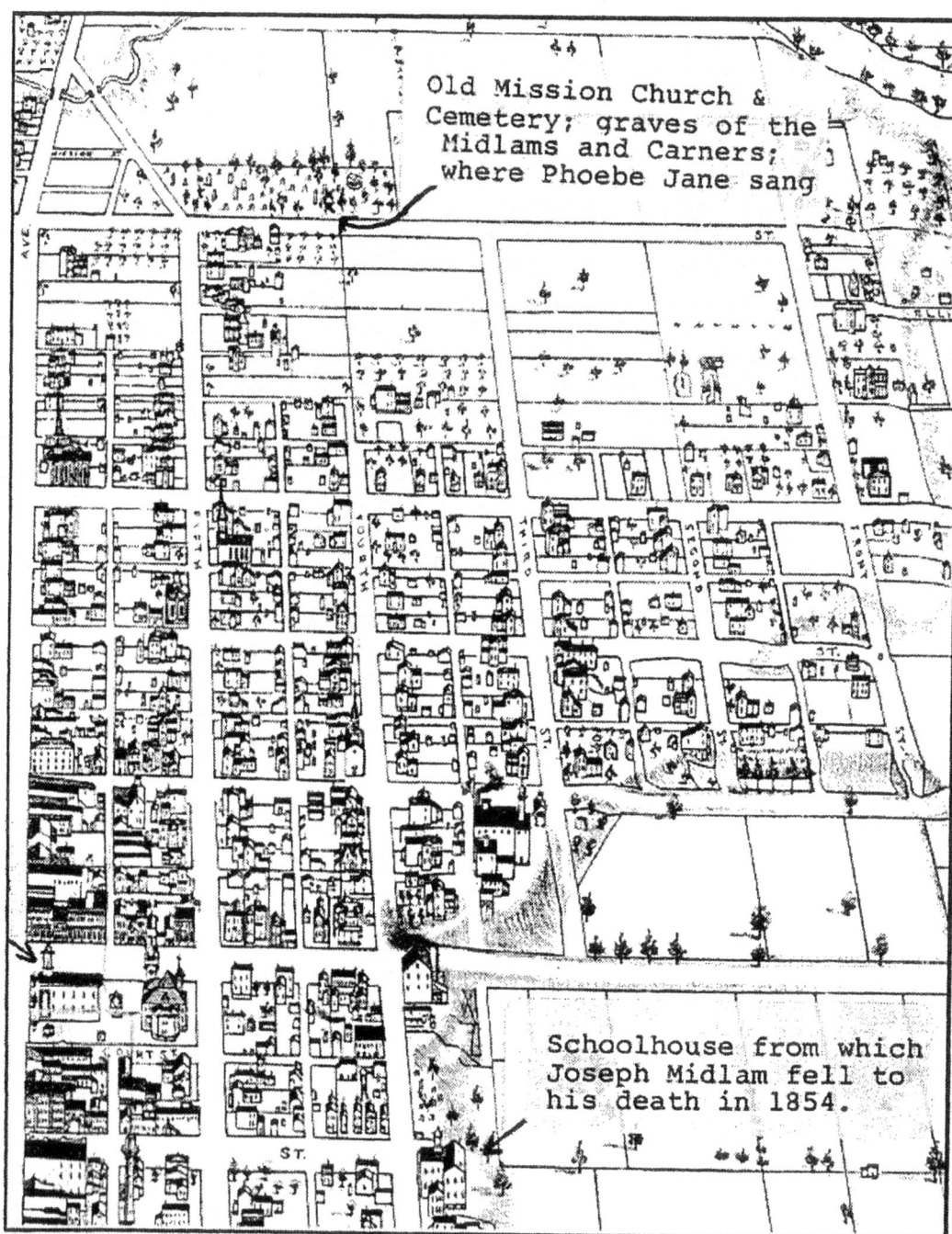

Maps in early county histories and atlases are invaluable and sometimes very well and accurately drawn. Here, from an early "Atlas Of Wyandot County, Ohio, is shown a party of the city of Upper Sandusky;" though highly stylized, the number, shape and position of the buildings shown were found to be very accurate. The schoolhouse from which the ancestor fell is here depicted in a very accurate way, as is the Old Mission Church. Such maps were truly works of art.

So, how do you solve the problem of knowing in what county records to look? It is very easy if you simply remember that unless the old county passed out of existence (became *extinct*) almost never were county records relating to land moved to a newly created county. That is, all new counties started from "scratch" with their own records. Thus, in whatever county you now find records of an ancestor, you will know that since its records commenced only at the date of its formation from other counties, you must look to the records of the earlier counties from which it was formed to continue backward through time.

Where do you look to learn the names of the old *predecessor counties*? In virtually all *county histories* (further of which later in this section), an early chapter will reveal what previous counties were carved up in order to bring that one into existence. In addition to that source, every state library has other and similar reading materials concerning the beginnings (the *genesis*) of its counties. Finally, numerous maps have been published showing boundary line changes which have taken place; such maps often keyed to the *Decennial Censuses*, which enumerations we will discuss shortly.

So, if you are to move backward in time you must learn of and do research within every one of the older counties which once had the power to tax and to govern the land occupied by a known ancestor. To not consider the genesis questions is to fail to do adequate research.

Books

Back to our discussion of the library. There, and of the greatest importance, you may expect to find the many works of previous historians and genealogists who have written family histories, histories of an area or county or state, and myriad other research aids. Those writers have *abstracted, extracted* from, compiled and summarized courts' records, ships' passengers and servants lists, church records, marriage bonds and ceremonies, lists of veterans, tax records of all kinds, land, deed, and mortgage records, wills and estates records, obituaries and cemetery lists, lists of noblemen such as earls and knights, and many, many other sources. Most of such works are well indexed, and you must thoroughly search those indexes for books and materials covering the time periods in which an ancestor is known to have lived.

How do you use a book? Never start with the index. Commence reading, instead, with the table of contents found in the front of the book. There you will learn how the book is organized and how the author thinks the subject matter should be broken down. Then read the Preface and Introduction. Within those sections you perhaps will learn which sources were included and, most importantly, which were not included, thus saving you many hours of searching through the indexes of books which contain no information that you need. If you have not done so, go now to the Table of Contents of this book and observe how this writer thinks the subject should be divided.

Citing Sources

Having found yourself amidst materials which are important to your search, it is absolutely necessary that you make a note of the *source* from which every bit of that information comes. It is not good enough that you believe (or, indeed, are most positive) that a fact is true. If you expect researchers and family members of the future to rely upon your findings and use the same as avenues to further research, you must set forth the source from which your information came; you must provide a *reference* for your reader. Especially will that be true later when you write of that ancestor or family line. You must cite the source, and even if the source is your own experience or is a tale told to you by a grandmother, that source should be spelled out. So, when you write down a new fact, also write down the source for that fact; not later, right then.

If your source is a written record, one of several acceptable ways to cite it is, first, to write down the name of the author and then the book title. Next, set forth the publisher and the year of that edition, and, finally, list the page or pages upon which you found the information used. For example:

Richard L. Morton, *Colonial Virginia*, 2 vols.; (University of North Carolina Press, Durham, 1960) Vol. 1, pp. 215—220.

It is not ever sufficient to cite, for example, "N. Car. Veterans records" or "Records of the D.A.R." You must be precise. You must provide your reader with enough information so that he or she may go seek out the same book and pages which you read and from which you quoted.

Notice also that if the information came from the Internet, you treat it in the same way as if it was found at the library. that is, list all the information found, and if the source was a person, supply as much information as possible about how that person may again be contacted. If the source was an institution, list the name and address as well as the URL (see glossary) of that institution. In short, note carefully the date, where you found the information, from whom or what institution, and any additional sources that person or site provided.

Searching For An Ancestor

You should choose but one or two names to research per trip to the library. Only when that library has been exhausted as to those names should you move to additional ancestors. Always resist the temptation to undertake the research of numerous names at the same time. Of course, if you are many miles from home you may need to search for a number of family names. Nevertheless, you still should start with but one and completely work it out before moving to others.

Just how do you undertake research of a certain ancestor or ancestral line? You need to know a name and an approximate time period. If you also know a place, you are that much ahead. Suppose you know that your grandmother was named Grace McCart before she married your grandfather John Sherrill. Also suppose you know that she died about 1950, when she was about eighty years old, and that before she was married she lived somewhere in or near Smith County, Illinois, the state in which you are now researching.

Censuses

The censuses will be very important to you and are a good place to begin. There has been a U.S. decennial census at the beginning of every decade since 1790, and therein may be found some record of most (notice that we said "most" and not "all") of those who were alive here when those censuses were taken. You will discover notable differences in the manner in which censuses were indexed in and after 1870, and much variation in the information to be gained from the different censuses. Generally speaking, the more recent the census the more information you will find here. As examples, the censuses taken in 1850 and thereafter listed the names and ages of all persons living within the household, usually their occupations, and some facts as to property they then owned, including any slaves. The slaves were not named.

However, the census for 1840 and the *enumerations* before then name only the *heads of households* (the men usually, or women if they were considered the dominant person of that residence), give only the numbers of other persons of both sexes within various age groups who were residing at that dwelling, usually provide information as to the number of slaves and servants, and but little else. So notice, for example, that if in 1840 (or at the taking of any other decennial census before that year) your ancestral great-grandmother lived with her daughter and son-in-law, she will be shown only as a female within a certain age group and will not be listed by name in any index to that census. That daughter and son-in-law will be found indexed under his *surname* (last name) and his *given name* (first name), which, of course, was different from that of the grandmother. The same also is true of their children; since they were not named, they are not indexed.

Other helpful census facts to remember are:
• The 1840 census listed U.S. Pensioners, thus providing clues to prior military or governmental service by a family member;
• the 1850 census (the first to name all members of the household) is the subject of many locations on the Internet where volunteers have set forth this very important material concerning their communities, counties or regions.
• except for a very few counties, the 1890 census was destroyed by fire and gross neglect, as were large parts of the census of 1790;
• the censuses of and after 1880 reveal the county and state of birth of the parents of the people listed;
• the censuses of 1900 and 1910 give the date of arrival of any immigrants there listed;
• and the 1920 census is the most recent one available since censuses are not open to the public for genealogical purposes until seventy-two years after their taking (the 1930 census will be opened to us in the year 2002).

Upon your first encounter with each of the many censuses, whether state or Federal, note carefully what information is to be found in the entries in that enumeration, and, as always, make a complete record of all of the family facts learned from those entries. Remember, when working with the decennial censuses be sure to use your printed forms. They are available for each national census since 1790 and are very helpful in record keeping and in citations of your sources. (The forms concerning the decennial censuses included in this book in Appendix 1, should be kept as "masters" and copied for future use.) As said, many libraries and bookstores also sell quite inexpensive census forms.

Genealogists and others have compiled and published indexes to the censuses taken before the number of people became so great as to make the publication of the complete censuses unwieldy and prohibitively expensive. Nevertheless, even where the numbers were great, many local societies have published indexes or the censuses themselves for their county or city. So it is that you usually will find both indexes and complete censuses by states for many of the enumerations through 1840, but after that the printed volumes may be indexed only, thus requiring you to view the microfilm if you want the total information available (and you do).

Indexes quite usually are titled, for example, *Index To The 1810 Census of Virginia*, and most libraries have printed censuses and indexes in the same section of the shelves. If you do not find them, ask the librarian for assistance.

When you find the name of an ancestor in the index to a census which has not been printed, you will need to go to the microfilm copy of the actual (original) census record to see the rest of the information. How do you do that? The *Index To The 1810 Census of Virginia*, for instance, relates simply that a man named "Keeler, William" is to be found at "016 Rcm." That notation means that a copy of the original entry concerning William Keeler and his family is on page 16 (016) of the census records of Rockingham County (Rcm) for that year. The library will have an alphabetized listing of the Virginia counties for that census, along with the microfilm roll numbers upon which those records will be found. Simply check out that microfilm roll (Rockingham 1810 happens to be roll #67) and, using the equipment—the *viewer*—available there at the library, move forward through it to page #16. There you will find both Keeler and the numbers of the others who then were within his household.

Be aware that since the original enumerations were done the censuses for many areas have been renumbered, sometimes several times, and the publishers of the index have utilized that enumeration which they believed to be the most recent. So, if your ancestor seems not to appear on the page listed in the index, carefully examine that page and the ones just preceding and just after for other and different sequences of page numbers. Through inadvertence, you may have moved forward through the reel in a sequence which was rendered obsolete by a later page numbering yet still is visible on the film. While census indexes are quite reliable in this regard, do be careful of page numbering (*pagination*).

Once you have found your ancestor in the microfilm record, it is very important to note whether or not the names found just before and just after that ancestor are in alphabetical order. Why? If not, they likely will then be in the same order as the enumerator (census taker) found them when he traveled the roads making the count. When the names are set forth as they were encountered, the neighbors on both sides are thus revealed. As with cemeteries, always make good notes as to those neighbors. Again, why? Because quite frequently (much more so in the early days than now) neighbors were relatives or in-laws and, furthermore, families from the same neighborhood or from a local church congregation often migrated west or south together, there again to live as neighbors. The Scots and Welsh were particularly known for living and moving in groups.

Interpreting Census Records

Back to our imaginary grandmother Grace McCart Sherrill. Because we know that she probably lived in Illinois and that she died about 1950 at near eighty years of age, we thereby may presume that Grace was born about 1870 (1950 minus 80 equals 1870), and since her maiden name was McCart, we might start with the 1880 U.S. census for Illinois. Remember too that in addition to the decennial censuses, there often were state censuses which are just as important for your purposes. Ask the librarian about the existence of such other enumerations; he or she will have a list of state censuses available or will direct you to the proper catalog heading or computer listing.

The indexes for the census of 1880 and thereafter are on computer, on a system called *Soundex*. With Soundex you need only type in the last name of your ancestor and the computer will tell you on which microfilm roll you can find him or her. A significant advantage of Soundex is that you do not need to know exactly how an ancestor's name was spelled to still be able to find him or her. Say, for example, that you cannot find McCart in the index because the enumerator misspelled it, or the name was originally spelled differently, or for whatever reason. You can then use Soundex to compile for you a list of all the names in the census that *sound* like McCart, such as McCurt, MacCardy, McCurdy etc., together with the microfilm roll and page number on which each appears. You can then look up each name until you find Grace and her family. The entry will give the names and details concerning the people found at that residence by the original enumerator. Soundex is easy to use, however rather than undertake here to memorize the method from this book, simply ask the librarian for assistance. Virtually all libraries have the Soundex code system set forth in an easy hand-out available for your use at the information desk.

In the 1880 Soundex you will find grandmother Grace as "McCart, Grace" (her maiden name). Suppose the 1880 entry shows Grace and her parents to have then resided in River Township of Smith County at residence "054." Check out the microfilm for that county for the year 1880, and at the beginning of that roll you will find the page number at which the entries for River Township commence. Move through the film to that page, and then move still further down the page to residence #54 where the details concerning the entire household with whom she then resided will be set forth.

Suppose that at residence #54 you find Grace to be a little girl of nine years of age. You now know that she probably was born in 1871 or thereabouts. As now, people often approximated ages, hence an age given in the census as "35" might in fact really be anywhere from thirty-four years and some months to very near thirty-six, depending upon the date the enumerator arrived at the house. That date is usually written at the top of each or every other page. Further, as with the other information, the ages may have been given by someone other than a parent, hence additional errors may be present due to mere lack of precise knowledge.

If Grace was living with her family, that 1880 census entry also should tell you 1) the names of Grace's parents or guardians, 2) their ages and occupations, 3) their birthplaces and, as mentioned, those of their parents (Grace's grandparents), 4) whether or not the adults there named were literate, 5) the relationship of each person living there to the head of the household, and 6) the dollar value given for both the real estate and the personal property owned by each person living within that household.

If they lived with Grace and her parents, her brothers and sisters (*siblings*) also will be listed. The eldest sibling quite usually will be listed first and the youngest last, with their birthplaces (*nativity*) and occupations set forth opposite their names. Note that if you find that the birthplace shown for one of the older children was different from that of a younger one, you have an excellent clue that during the period of time between the birth of those two children the family moved from the earlier birthplace to the later one. As an example, you might find that in the 1860 census for Louisiana your ancestors, Wayne and Laura, were the parents of Alex, born in 1852 in Alabama, and that their next child was Sam, he shown as having been born in Louisiana in 1854. Thereby you have strong evidence that the family moved from Alabama to Louisiana sometime during the years 1852 (when Alex was born) and 1854 (when Sam was born). Thus, such information sends you to Alabama and the 1850 census to pick up the trail before then and to continue your search.

Moving Backwards In Time

Remember always that by simply subtracting the age of the eldest child named from the year of that census, you will have an approximate year before which the marriage of the parents likely took place. So, if Grace's eldest brother was shown by the census of 1880 to have been seventeen years old, by subtracting 17 from 1880 we arrive at the year 1863 as the probable year of his birth, hence also the year during or before which we should expect to find the marriage of his parents. In that regard, note that they may never have married; some did not. Nevertheless, by your subtraction you still will have ascertained an approximate year during which they began their lives together. Note also that the records of many marriages were not preserved, hence will never be found.

Speaking further of siblings (brothers and sisters): make careful notes of their given names, especially if you have found those same names elsewhere in the family. Just as today, recurring names were common, and very few families failed to name at least one child after a parent, aunt, uncle or ancestor. While you now may not be particularly interested in such collateral lines (families of brothers and sisters and their in-laws and spouses and descendants of cousins), should you later choose to write of the family you quite likely will want to include and index their names. Further, it is probable that among the descendants of those siblings, you will find other persons researching your family. Few indeed are the families within which there has not been previous research.

As noted, in years past just as now, many children were named after their parents, grandparents, or others in the family who were well liked or highly regarded, hence a recurring name within a family line may reveal to you an ancestor from whom that name first came. Perhaps no better illustration may be found than in the case of a Richard Parker who lived in Virginia in the mid 1600s (the *seventeenth century*). Since the first Richard, there has been a Parker named that in that family for at least nine generations. So too, the families of the patriots George Mason and Terry Connor and the Saltonstalls of New England.

Suppose the 1880 census microfilm reveals opposite his name that the birthplace of Grace's father was Edgecombe County, North Carolina, and that of her mother was Bourbon County, Kentucky. You now have a running start on that branch of the family, and after completing your Smith County work, you may continue your search for her mother in the Bourbon County and Kentucky research materials, and for her father in those for Edgecombe County and eastern North Carolina.

In that 1880 census you will also learn the ages of Grace's parents. Like with her brothers and sisters, by simply subtracting those ages given from 1880, you also have their approximate birth years. (Be cautious however, for the names, numbers, and dates found in censuses are only as reliable as the enumerators and the persons who provided the information to those enumerators.) Through those differing birthplaces of the father and mother, you also may have a clue concerning the location of the marriage records for that couple. As did many, when yet a young man the father may have gone from North Carolina to Kentucky, there met and married Grace's mother, after which they went to the Illinois country together. Notice that since most early migration was from east to west and south, not vice versa, it would be most unlikely (yet not unheard of) that the marriage took place back in North Carolina.

So check the records for Smith County, and if you do not find the marriage of Grace's parents there you then should move to the Kentucky marriages, all the while remembering that the parents may never have married, or the record of that union may now be lost. If the library being searched has no further materials concerning marriages or other records of either Kentucky or North Carolina, put your notes aside as to those members of the family. You can take that search up later in other libraries which contain more materials as to those states.

After finishing the 1880 census search, move backwards in time; check the census for 1870 next. Notice that if neither Grace nor her family appear in the 1870 census for Smith County, then they probably moved from Kentucky or wherever to Illinois during the years between those censuses; 1870—1880. As we said—and it is important—the approximate year and state or location from which their move took place may be revealed by the birthplaces of the children listed. An example: if a three-year-old child was said in the 1880 census to have been born in Kentucky, yet a one-year-old sister of that child was shown to have been born in Illinois, the period between 1878 and 1880 probably was that during which the move took place. So, think!

Having established that their move probably took place in the 1870s, you may pick up the trail by checking 1870 and the earlier censuses in those previous states— Kentucky and before that North Carolina—from which places you now suspect that the family came.

After you have moved backwards through the available censuses—1860, 1850, 1840, etc.—to the point at which Grace and her family no longer appear, go back again to 1880 and start moving forward through the years to 1900, 1910, etc. (remember; the 1890 census is probably missing), again making complete notes as to all information gained.

Reliability of Census Information

Concerning the reliability of census information, as the census takers arrived at the homes of the citizens, oftentimes the man of the house was working in the fields or was away from home, and if the wife also was out of the house, the enumerator may have gotten the family details and information from a child or even from a boarder, live-in, or neighbor. Further, then as now, many people, including some census takers, were not conscientious and careful. Then too, most of our ancestors were known to take a drink on a hot day to cool down, or on a cold day to warm themselves. In fact, nearly everyone drank intoxicants (more by reason of an abiding distrust of the water than from a desire to be drunk, it must be said, even though, as now, that urge often was close at hand). Some enumerators were lazy, inept, or anxious to return home. So, for the reasons given, errors regularly crept into census returns.

Illiteracy

It also is important to remember that in the early days a great many folks were illiterate, hence the enumerators who came by often were required to provide the *phonetic* (how it sounded) spelling of the names told to them. Were that not problem enough, the enumerators themselves quite often had very limited education. So, make careful notes of any spelling variations found, and be aware that an ancestor, especially an illiterate one, may be found in a census under a spelling different from both the earlier and the later censuses. In the censuses after 1850 the literacy of those in the household was stated.

Other Factors Causing Errors

Quill pens (usually made from the prime tail feathers of geese), while the best writing instruments then available, nevertheless worked sporadically at best, and sometimes not at all. Especially evident are such failings when the movement of the hand was straight to either the left or to the right. Thus, a capital (upper case) letter such as "R" may appear as a "K" and "O" might look like a "U" or even as "II". An example: In an 1860 Ohio census, William R. Drake appears quite clearly as William K. Drake, the left to right top of the letter R having been skipped by the pen.

In addition, sometimes the ink used was of very poor quality and the handwriting even worse. Examples of incorrect and misleading census information are known to every researcher, and soon you too will have uncovered misleading data concerning one or more ancestors. So, always be aware of the likelihood of unintentional error, and intentional as well, as where a measure of shame was present over illegitimacy, criminal activity, etc., or where a member of the family desired that his or her whereabouts not be known.

Boarders and Live-ins

As to boarders and other live-ins, keep in mind that in the early days many, perhaps even most, rural homes (and many urban households, as well) sheltered and maintained farm hands, servants and others who, though not members of the immediate family, also were not slaves. Such folks were enumerated with that family. Further, families very often provided a home for aged parents—usually the mother, but sometimes both mother and father—and for *spinster* (unmarried) aunts and disabled or handicapped relatives. Then too, and often, especially before the period 1840—1850, children were *fostered out* or *apprenticed* to another family, these children usually being required to provide a helping hand to the households having charge of them, and also thereby relieving the birth-parents of the financial and physical burden of raising these children. Quite usually, the new family agreed to provide such children with training in some trade or calling in exchange for the labor of the children.

Folks who were neither the parents nor children of the heads of household were listed following the names of those prime members. In such cases, even though again, errors were made, the prescribed order for listing was, first, head of household, then his (or her) spouse, followed by their children beginning with the eldest and continuing through the youngest, next the parents of the head of household, then parents of the spouse, then other relatives, and lastly, any live-ins and boarders, again, with the eldest shown first.

By reason of the likelihood of live-ins, in the censuses prior to 1850 where only the heads of households were specifically named, when you find in any age group a larger number of people than would make sense in light of your other research, you have probably uncovered such boarders and non-direct family members. Make careful notes of the names or ages of all such live-ins. Even if they were not then, they later may have become relatives through marriage to a member of that family.

Origins of Surnames

The origin of the surname of any ancestor is sometimes important to you. By realizing that Grace was born a "McCart," you have a clue as to her background; that is, a clue to her father's lineage. The name "McCart" is almost surely Scottish, hence her *paternal* (her father's side) ancestors quite probably once were Scottish or Scotch-Irish. The prefixes Mac- and Mc- meant "son of." So too, in Wales and Ireland; the ap- in Welsh names (ap-Griffith) and the O'- in Irish names (O'Neal) both meant "son of" (son of Griffith, son of Neal).

So, how will you find such places of origin? Either in the genealogical section or in the general reference section in nearly all libraries you will find books which discuss the histories and derivations of surnames. Look up each and every one of your family names therein, and then, not sometime later, for your future use, make good notes on that family unit chart concerning the nationality and meaning of the name. Having learned that the McCarts likely originated in Scotland, in later searching you likely will come to seek out and utilize materials having to do with that nation and its people. Having learned of such nations of origin, by using one of the *search engines* (see glossary) we discussed in Chapter 3, you can type in the name of the country about which you want to learn, and so come to know those lands of ancestors and of the people that did and do inhabit those places.

The Spelling of Names

It is very important that you always remember that over the many centuries virtually every family name has been spelled in different ways. (If you want to reveal that you are a novice and new to this hobby, all you need to do is insist to an experienced researcher that your family spelled your surname in only one way.) So, be most cautious and do not assume that simply because your grandmother spelled her name in a certain way that anyone else before (or after) her did the same. For example, McCart probably once was McCarty or McCarthy or MacCardy or even McCurdy; Beatty may have been Batte, Baty, Beattie, or Beaty; the German surname Feldstein may now be Fieldstone; Schmidt may be Smith, Smithe, or Smythe, or a dozen other spellings; Blanco may now be White, and Moreno, now Brown. German names such as Knertzer may now be Kornetzer, Conatser, or Cornester; Koerner may now be Carner or Kerner or Korner or even Connor; Kessler may have been Kistler, Kestler, or Kiessler; and Schneider likely is now Snyder, yet may be Schneiter, Schneyder, Snider, or even Taylor (tailor), which is what Schneider means in German.

Then too, do not forget that for given names contractions and nicknames were used then, just as now, e.g., Jane may have been Jenny; Veronica (sounded like "Fronica" in German) often was Fronny or Franny or even Frances; Elizabeth became Betsy, Betty, Beth, Liz, Lizzy, or Libby; Rebecca was Beck or Becky; Tabitha commonly was Tabby; Bill, Billy, Will, or Willie served for William; Tommy or Tom for Thomas; Lafe for Lafayette; Hank or Harry may have been Henry; John was Jack many times, and on and on. So, always be alert for nicknames!

It also is important that you remember that the terms Sr. (Senior) and Jr. (Junior) may have meant only that a certain person was the older or the younger of two people with the same name living in the same neighborhood, and the two may not have been related at all. Note that, unlike now, those terms also occasionally were used when referring to women as well as men. The words sister and brother often were used in the Biblical sense and did not refer to kinship, especially in letters and other correspondence. Then too, in the early days in-law was not a term of precise meaning and often was used when identifying step-parents, adopted children, or those who had a guardian. Cousin very often meant any relative more distant than parent or brother or sister, and just as now, children were taught to show respect by addressing such older cousins, other relatives, and even friends of the family as aunt or uncle. So, be very careful!

Cousins and "Greats"

Cousin type relationships are not difficult to figure out, and much ado has been made and nonsense written about what is really a very simple reckoning. If you and another relative have one or more common grandparents, you are first cousins. The children of such first cousins are your first cousins, once removed, and are not your second cousins. Likewise, your children are the first cousins, once removed of your first cousins. Your second cousins are those people who share with you one or more common great-grandparents. Your third cousins are those people who share one or more common great-great grandparents. So, simply count the number of greats in the title of the most recent common ancestor and add one (1), and you have the degree of cousinhood. Thus, if your third-great grandfather is the most recent common ancestor of you and another person, then you and that person are fourth cousins. That person's children are your fourth cousins, once removed, and that person's grandchildren are your fourth cousins, twice removed.

Relationships of remote aunts and uncles are determined in the same easy way. Simply take the number of greats in an ancestor's name and add one (1) more great before the word "aunt" or "uncle" when speaking of the brothers and sisters of that ancestor. So, if a person was the sister of your grandmother (there are zero (0) "greats" in your grandmother's name), add one (1) great, and she is your great-aunt (also sometimes called grand-aunt). If a man was a brother of your great-grandfather (there is one (1) great in the grandfather's title) add one more great for a total of two (2), and that brother is your great-great uncle. So, the sister of your fourth-great grandmother was your fifth-great aunt, and so on. Incidentally, do not bore or wear out your listeners by describing an ancestor as, for example, "my great-great-great-great-great grandmother." If it is important to the conversation, say "my fifth-great grandmother," if not, say simply "my ancestor."

Birth, Adoptive, and Foster Parents

If you or an ancestor were adopted or fostered out, there are ways of disentangling the prior records and learning something—often a great deal—about the birth-parents and their ancestors. The means and methods for conducting such searches are the subject of several good books and are beyond the scope of this work. Still though, remember that the best first approach to such research problems is geographical in nature. Gain all information possible as to WHERE the adopted or fostered child, the suspected birth-parents, and the adoptive or foster parents lived during the years immediately before and immediately after the birth date of the child. Your search will begin with interviews of officials and in the courthouses and hospitals in those areas.

If you come upon such relationships during your research, make careful notes and glean every fact and bit of information possible from those you are interviewing and from everybody else having any knowledge whatever of the facts. In genealogical problem solving, no bit of information is too small or insignificant to be carefully noted. Surely, that is even more true with adoption or foundling problems.

Titles And Forms Of Address

Finally in the matter of how our ancestors were addressed: in the 17th and early 18th centuries the terms *Mr.* and *Mrs.* were important titles and were used only when addressing or referring to persons who had gained (or inherited) position, wealth, and great respect within their community. So, only if their contemporaries did so should you refer to an ancestor as either Mr. or Mrs. Often two persons with the same name may be distinguished one from the other by learning that one was addressed as Mr. while the other was not. Always remember the expression "Same name does not mean same person."

Incidentally, all early public offices were considered worthwhile and important and were sought after vigorously, hence when you find an ancestor who was, for example, a *Burgess, Justice of the Peace,* or *Constable,* you may be assured that he or she was held in considerable regard by his contemporaries and peers. Further, such persons very often were referred to as Mr. or Mrs., at least while in that position, even if they were not so addressed before and after occupying the office.

Researching Through The Use of Ages

Try always to reason and to think through the years of an ancestor's life. If, as in our example, in the 1880 Census you found Grace McCart to have been nine years old, you know that she probably was born in about the year 1871 (written as circa 1871, or

c. 1871, or c1871). Hence there is no point in searching for her name in records considerably before that year. Nor will she be found in any marriage records before the mid-1880s, since she was but a child during the years prior to then. Moreover, she will not be found signing documents nor paying taxes before about 1890, since she was not yet of mature years. If you learn that she had a son born in 1910, yet do not know her death date, there surely is no point in searching for her among death and estate records before the year of the birth of her child. Remember, though, that she may appear by name at any age in church records and in all the censuses after 1840. By determining a span of years during which an event MUST have happened, you have eliminated the need to search for that event in the many records and books for those years during which that happening could not have taken place.

Speaking of ages, while quite usually anyone who was *tithable* was over sixteen, it is important to remember that in the very early years the expression *of age* did not necessarily mean that a person was eighteen or twenty-one years old. Of age or *of majority* often meant that his or her peers and the lawgivers of that day considered the person mature and able to act as an adult, regardless of the number of his or her years. Hence, while a child of six almost surely would not ever be viewed as of age, a twelve-year-old might. Only during the last century did the law of most states uniformly determine that twenty-one (or eighteen, sometimes) was of age. Be aware also that for a very long time fourteen was (and in some places still is) an age at which children could enter into various contractual relationships and make many decisions affecting their relationships with their parents, guardians, and with the world.

So, while researching, always stop and think through the problem. Pretend that you are the person being researched, such as Grace, and were born in 1871 or whenever. Then start looking in the books and materials which relate to the appropriate periods in the life of that person.

When researching someone's life in a certain state, such as Grace in Illinois, you must thoroughly search for the name in all the records for that period of time between her birth and her death or the year in which she is known to have left that county or state. Further, it is wise to check the indexes for a few years after the death or known removal of that person from the state, since proceedings having to do with *estates* or inheritances from other states may not have been filed nor appear of record until sometime—often many years—later.

Time Line Drawings

While researching, simple *time line drawings* are immensely helpful to your thinking and organization of materials. On the back of that family unit chart dedicated to Grace and her husband draw a straight line for each of those marriage partners. Put their birth dates and years near the left ends of those lines and their death dates near the right ends. Divide the lines into five year periods, and each time you learn a new fact or anecdote about either of them, briefly note that information at the proper year on their time line. By so doing, a bit at a time, you will find yourself able to reconstruct a most interesting life story of Grace and her family, and the small effort involved in making such drawings also will help you remember the facts concerning that family. Always remember that genealogy is the study of lives, events, and emotions, and is not a mere gathering of names and dates.

On the backs of their family unit charts, do a similar time line sketch for each of your ancestors. Incidentally, the back of the unit chart is a fine (perhaps the best) place to write both new facts and the corresponding references concerning the members of that family unit.

Departments of Vital Statistics

After the beginning of the twentieth century (the 1900's), our states established departments to house and maintain *vital statistics*—"vita" is Latin for "life"—and vital statistics are those statistics which relate to birth, death, marriage, health and disease. States established departments of vital records at different times, so be sure to check the state in which you are interested. As an example, with the exception of only a few cities Virginia began this mandatory recording on June 14, 1912, while Tennessee did not do so till later in that decade.

Despite such rules instituted by the state governments, for some years thereafter more than a few local officials and physicians ignored or forgot to submit information concerning these such records, and as a result, even though the law where they lived might have required it, for some years after the births and deaths of some ancestors their records may not have found their way into the states' records.

These departments of government are most important to the researcher, and by addressing a letter to the Bureau of Vital Statistics at your state capital you may procure a form which, though variously named, when filled out and returned, will provide such data as is available for the birth or the death of a particular ancestor. To utilize this source and gain *birth certificates* and *death certificates* by mail you quite usually need to know the exact date of the event (birth or death). However in most states you may visit in person, use their computerized indexes (set forth by years or groups of years) and, upon locating the ancestor, order the printed information which will be sent to you later. The charge is usually very reasonable.

Depending upon whether you seek data concerning a birth or a death, you likely will find considerable information here, often including date and place of birth, parents' names, marriage dates, cause, place, and date of death, persons present, and perhaps the birthplaces and facts concerning next of kin and parents.

So, for anyone who died after the early years of the twentieth century, you might start your search by utilizing these very valuable vital statistics. Since Grace died in 1950, if you knew the date and in what state she died, you could have written for a copy of the death certificate at the same time at which you started your census work concerning her life. Funeral homes also often have kept records of customers over many years, recording times of deaths, funerals, interments, who purchased the services, etc. These records are usually found in the library of the town or county in which such businesses formerly operated and are well known to the local historical or genealogical society (of which below). They always should be checked for all family members who lived and died during the periods covered by the records.

CERTIFICATE OF DEATH
COMMONWEALTH OF VIRGINIA
DEPARTMENT OF HEALTH, BUREAU OF VITAL STATISTICS

1. PLACE OF DEATH		2. USUAL RESIDENCE
a. COUNTY	b. MAGISTERIAL DISTRICT	a. STATE Virginia b. COUNTY
c. CITY OR TOWN Norfolk	d. IS PLACE OF DEATH INSIDE CITY LIMITS? YES ☒ NO ☐	c. CITY OR TOWN Norfolk d. IS RESIDENCE INSIDE CITY LIMITS? YES ☒ NO ☐
c. HOSPITAL OR INSTITUTION Norfolk General Hospital	f. LENGTH OF STAY	e. STREET (If rural, give mailing address) 5601 Lenoir Circle f. IS RESIDENCE ON A FARM? YES ☐ NO ☒

3. NAME OF DECEASED (Type or Print)			4. DATE OF DEATH
a. (First) WILLIAM	b. (Middle) CAMERON	c. (Last) GROVE	(Month) (Day) (Year) March 8, 1956

5. SEX Male	6. COLOR OR RACE White	7. MARRIED ☒ NEVER MARRIED ☐ WIDOWED ☐ DIVORCED ☐	8. DATE OF BIRTH May 18, 1912	9. AGE 43	Months 9 Days 20 Hours Min

10a. USUAL OCCUPATION Warehouse Man	10b. KIND OF BUSINESS OR INDUSTRY Naval Base	11. BIRTHPLACE Goshen, Virginia	12. CITIZEN OF WHAT COUNTRY USA

13. FATHER'S NAME William Cameron Grove, Sr.	14. MOTHER'S MAIDEN NAME Daisy Drake

15. NAME OF HUSBAND OR WIFE OF DECEASED Nan Mulvaney Grove	16. SOCIAL SECURITY NO.	17. INFORMANT'S SIGNATURE Mrs. A. R. Miller ADDRESS Norfolk, Virginia

18. CAUSE OF DEATH	INTERVAL BETWEEN ONSET AND DEATH
PART I. DEATH WAS CAUSED BY: IMMEDIATE CAUSE (a) Acute Coronary thrombosis	Minutes
Conditions, if any, which gave rise to above cause (a), stating the underlying cause last. DUE TO (b) Coronary Sclerosis	Unknown
DUE TO (c)	
PART II. OTHER SIGNIFICANT CONDITIONS CONTRIBUTING TO DEATH BUT NOT RELATED TO THE TERMINAL DISEASE CONDITION GIVEN IN PART I (a)	19. WAS AUTOPSY PERFORMED? YES ☐ NO ☒

20a. ACCIDENT ☐ SUICIDE ☐ HOMICIDE ☐	20b. DESCRIBE HOW INJURY OCCURRED
20c. TIME OF INJURY	
20d. INJURY OCCURRED WHILE AT WORK ☐ NOT WHILE AT WORK ☐	20e. PLACE OF INJURY 20f. CITY, TOWN, OR LOCATION COUNTY STATE

21. I attended the deceased from _____ to _____ and last saw _____ March 8, 1956
Death occurred at 7:50 P. m. on the date stated above; and to the best of my knowledge, from the causes stated

22a. SIGNATURE Chas. O. Barclay, Jr., M.D. (Degree or title) Med.Exam.	22b. ADDRESS Portsmouth, Virginia	22c. DATE SIGNED 3-12-56

23a. BURIAL, CREMATION, REMOVAL (Specify) Removal	23b. DATE 3-10-56	23c. NAME OF CEMETERY OR CREMATORY Transportation via hearse to Richmond, Va. 23d. LOCATION

DATE REC'D BY LOCAL REG. 3/13/56	REGISTRAR'S SIGNATURE J. C. Craft	24. FUNERAL DIRECTOR'S SIGNATURE Hollomon-Brown Funeral Home, Inc. Norfolk, Virginia

Here, from the office of Vital Statistics of the State of Virginia, is the "Death Certificate" of W. C. Grove, Sr., who died suddenly in Virginia in 1956. It contains the cause of death, the names of his parents, and many other facts that are very important to a researcher.

Genealogical Clubs and Societies

Any librarian will be glad to tell you of the local genealogical societies and clubs, and even if you live many miles away, you should join a society that serves an area where you have several ancestors or family lines. There are many such societies, and membership is not expensive. Such organizations are made up of folks just like you, and quite usually they publish a newsletter or periodical, many of which will provide you with opportunities to run small ads (known as *queries*) seeking others who are researching family lines and ancestors that are common to you.

Don't forget that the Internet can provide you with the names and addresses of most of the genealogical clubs and societies that you might want to join. Remember too, many such organizations will allow you to join, subscribe to their newsletters, pose queries, or request information through e-mail alone. Sometimes, if you are lucky and someone from the society is at their computer, you may have an answer to your questions very quickly. Whether from ordinary mail or e-mail, often a single exchange of correspondence will extend a family line for several generations, especially when you are new to the hobby. Many new and interesting friends will also thereby be made.

When writing a letter to be mailed to others, courtesy and custom dictate that you always include a self-addressed, stamped envelope (called an *SASE*) which the recipient of your inquiry may use in responding to you. In your correspondence (and at all other times, for that matter) never hesitate to ask questions of other researchers. They too have had to solve difficult problems and usually will help. Unfortunately and occasionally you will encounter a researcher who will not help you. There are those who apparently feel that since they had to do the research, so should you. Never adopt that attitude. If we all did, research would be next to impossible.

Warning: Never think that you know so much that others can not help you, especially if you are at a "dead end" and are unable to go beyond some prior point in time. Finally, remember always that answers received from other researchers by mail, e-mail, telephone or word of mouth are only as reliable as are the people doing the writing or speaking, so always check all answers and sources for yourself.

In addition to the local societies, all states have genealogical and historical societies—again accessible through the Internet—that are most helpful in research and in uncovering historical background and ancestry; the *Virginia Genealogical Society Journal* is but one of many. There also are regional and national organizations such as the *Tidewater Genealogical Society* and the *National Genealogical Society*; again, both of great value. Such large organizations nearly all maintain a website and publish very scholarly materials. If you can afford it, join one of these organizations which work in the larger perspective.

Then too, there are numerous private publishers of magazines of general interest to genealogists, but two of which are *Genealogical Helper* (Everton Publishers Inc., Logan, UT) and *Heritage Quest* (Orting, WA) (see also Appendix 3). Most libraries and many people who do family research are or have been subscribers and usually will be happy to give you a subscription form for either. Finally in the matter of publications, you will find many publications and websites dedicated to specific families, especially those with the more common surnames like Wright, Johnson, Jones, Smith, etc., or devoted to geographical areas or counties, e.g., The Rowan County Register (Ms. Jo White Linn,

Salisbury, NC). Sometime, before long, you may even want to start your own such letter or journal or web-site.

In certain cases you might even want to consider calling in the assistance of a professional researcher. Such researchers are to be found in every area, often have websites or advertise in periodicals such as those mentioned above, and will be glad to assist you for usually reasonable hourly rates. Nearly always, however, your own research will be more rewarding and probably less expensive. Caution: many who advertise their services are not as capable of searching the records as you now are, so never fail to ask for and contact references before hiring professionals. True professionals are proud of their expertise and accomplishments and will be happy to supply credentials.

Local Materials

In addition to the standard works, every library has some materials that are unique to that area and, thus, of much importance to you. Most librarians are proud of their collections and happy to discuss their materials with you. So ask them to tell you about their local records. Then, just as with your interviews, you listen and let them talk.

There is a vast quantity of local material. For example, after the invention of the typesetting machine and during the last thirty years of the nineteenth century (1800s), it became fashionable (just as now) for counties and some cities to publish books concerning their history, people and places. Such local histories contained maps (particularly valuable) and drawings of homes (usually highly stylized, however numbers and the nature of buildings located on the properties often may be determined), anecdotes, biographies, and many other interesting facts. But, caution: Remember that the dates and details to be found in the biographical and genealogical portions of such publications quite usually were the products of the memories of those then living who usually were not genealogists, and thus errors very often were made. So, as with all materials and facts from derivative sources, be very careful and skeptical, and always confirm the information learned through other perhaps more reliable source materials.

As suggested earlier, you may check these local histories to learn from which other counties that county was carved; to learn of its genesis. If you find that in 1871 Smith County was formed from part of Madison County, then, as we have learned, Grace's parents may appear before 1871 in the records of Madison County without ever having moved.

Take the time to check local newspapers published during the three or four week period following a significant event in the life (or death) of an ancestor. Even though the original newspapers may yet exist and be found in the archives of the newspaper, the county, or the state, more often than not they are on microfilm and available in many libraries in the area. There you may find an *obituary*, a short life description, or an article concerning a marriage which reveals important and interesting facts previously quite unknown to you. Always gain copies of such discoveries. Keep in mind, as is true of published county histories, as a general rule newspapers were (and are) not historically terribly reliable. Those publishers were trying to market newspapers at a profit, not recording history. So exercise caution, and, as always, check your findings against more reliable sources.

In nearly all libraries you will find a group of files indexed by family name, often called *vertical files* or *family name files*. Therein will be found clippings, letters to the library from others searching the same surnames, and written materials given to or collected by the library, most of which pertain to local families. Ask the librarian if there are such family name files, and if so, never fail to examine them. Such files will be in alphabetical order by surname. Be sure to submit copies of your own materials and findings for inclusion there, in order that those who come after you also may have an easier task. Again, the materials found in such family name files are only as reliable as were the writers, and often are not carefully done. So, be skeptical and check the sources cited.

THE RESIDENT TAX-PAYERS OF 1810.

John Agnew, John Allen, Samuel Adams, John Adams,[12] Joseph Buterbaugh, Aaron Bush, Jacob Bushlock, Sebastian Bushlock, Peter Brewer, John Bard, Dr. John Buchanan,[13] Absalom Bayles, Henry Bucher, George Bechtel, John Brubaker, Stephen Brothers, Michael Bradbaugh, John Bels, Joseph Christy, William Crawford, Benjamin Castlebarger, Samuel Craig, Jacob Condron, John Cunningham, Abraham Cumbaker, Peter Clossin, John Christy, John Conntz, James Condron, Jacob Cramer, Peter Casshly,[14] George Cramer,[15] Patrick Cassidy, Andrew Childester, Edward Dougherty, David Davis, Samuel Donner, Richard Drury, Michael Fetter, John Forrester, Robert Felton, Harmon Ferber,[16] George Foglesong,[17] Paul Frazier, John Grove, Christian Ghost, Christian Garber,[18] Jacob Garman, George Gibson, Peter Gear, Andrew Henderson (for Hollidaysburg), Andrew Hildebrandt,[19] John Hogh, John Haines, Michael Hileman, Jr., Peter Hetrick, Michael Hileman, Sr.,[20] John Hileman, Mary Holliday, (widow) John Holliday, William Holliday, Benjamin Henley, Francis Henry, Robert Hamilton, Jacob Hazel, Patrick Hamilton, Philip Hetrick, Anthony Hileman, John Holliday (major), James Irwin, James Irwin, Jr., John Irwin, Peter Lsenour, Jared Irwin, John Irwin, William Jones, David Jones, Jenkins Jones, Evan Jones, Sarah Jeck, Henry K. Ketner, Henry Kisner, Lud-

---

1 Tavern-keeper.	2 Tavern-keeper.
	3 Owned a saw-mill.
4 Tavern-keeper.	5 Owned a grist-mill.
6 Owned one slave, one saw-mill, and seven hundred acres of land.	
7 Tavern-keeper.	8 Owners of slaves.
9 Owned grist- and saw-mills.	10 Owned a saw-mill each.
11 Probably intended for *Rench*.	12 Tavern-keeper.
13 Practicing physician.	14 Owned a saw-mill.
15 Owned a distillery.	16 Owned a distillery.
17 Owned two distilleries.	18 Owned two distilleries.
19 Owned a distillery.	20 Owned a distillery.

From local materials, here is a list containing information probably no longer available from any other source. From a 19th-century history of Huntingdon and Blair Counties, Pennsylvania; a list of resident taxpayers in Holidaysburg in 1810.

MADISON

Scale 1¾ inches to the Mile

R. 21   T. 10

From Atlas of Pickaway County, 1871.

Tract owned in 1804 by Broad Cole, grand-father of Susannah Cole Drake.

Tract owned from 1846 to 1852 by Demmitt Cole. W. K. Drake believed to have lived here.

ST. PAUL'S P.O.

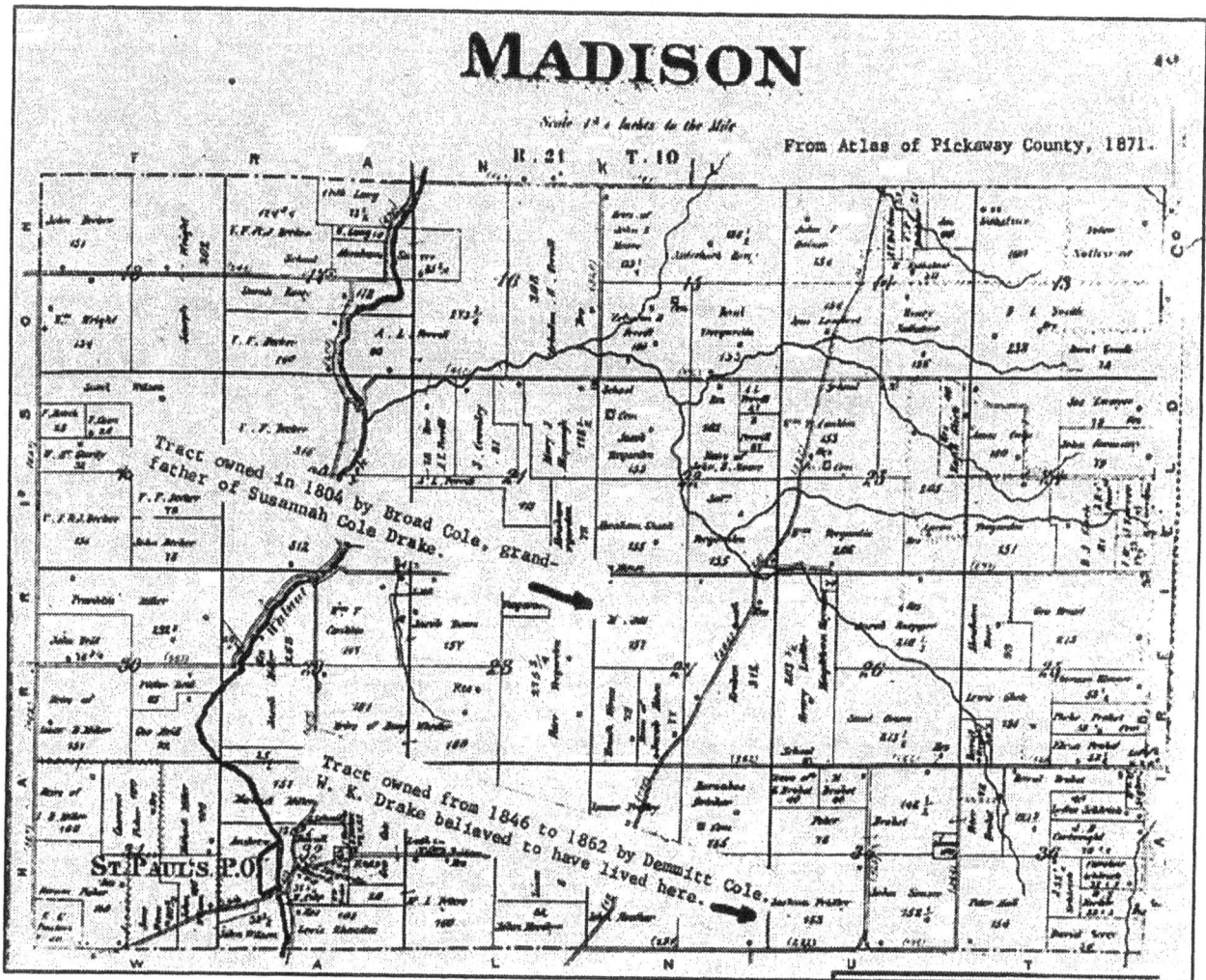

As are other valuable finds, landowner maps found in local materials are often extremely valuable to researchers. Here, from an 1871 "Atlas of Pickaway County, Ohio" are found the landowners of Madison Township at that time. A wonderful discovery for a researcher who finds the property of his or her ancestor drawn here.

Genealogical Periodicals

Speaking of matters indexed by surnames, you must not ignore the myriad articles concerning families and their activities which have been written and published in the many *periodicals* (the magazines of history and genealogy) to which reference has already been made. Such fine publications as *The New York Genealogical and Biographical Record*, *The Virginia Genealogist*, *The William and Mary Quarterly*, and *The Vermont Historical Society Journal* have annual and also cumulative indexes, websites, and over the past one hundred fifty years have identified or discussed tens of thousands of our ancestors.

Simply locate those periodicals on the library shelves, and if they are not apparent to you ask the librarian where the indexes to such publications may be found. These sources are very valuable! Never decide that your family was not important enough to have been mentioned in magazines and journals; chances are you will find several ancestors there.

Soon, thanks to the efforts of many, and to your own work as well, you will find yourself searching in colonial America. "Colonial" refers to the period and events prior to the end of the American Revolution (1783), during which we were colonies of England, France, Spain, Holland, etc.

Things were different then; we were English men and women, had kings and queens instead of presidents; had royal governors instead of elected ones; permitted only male landowners to vote; approved of slave ownership in nearly all colonies (but only a few folks owned or needed any); used mostly pounds (£), shillings (s) and pence (p), but also used French, Spanish, Dutch, and Indian money (wampum) as well as tobacco and other commodities as currency; knew virtually nothing of medicine and so died of the most common ailments (smallpox, yellow fever, malaria, pleurisy, flu, any puncture wound of the chest or abdomen, virtually all gunshot wounds, etc.); ate extremely well if wealthy, and quite poorly if not so; had those who were well off and those who were poor, and almost no middle class; hunted for much of our meat and fish, and raised or bartered for the rest; heated and cooked with wood over an open fireplace; considered a husband and wife as one person, and that person was the man; believed in spirits, ghosts, apparitions, and that some people arose from the dead; either disliked or distrusted American Indians; jailed people who could not pay their debts; and punished criminals with a severity now beyond our wildest imagination.

Such differences are incredibly interesting, will be encountered as you research, and should be included in the story of your family. And, if you find an interest in such matters, many good books are available. Simply check the catalog at the library under the heading "American colonies" and "colonial life" or search the many book sellers on the Internet.

Indentured Servants, Redemptioners, And Criminals

Many—in fact, over 200,000—of our colonial ancestors were *indentured servants*. Another 40,000 came here as *redemptioners*—for our purposes, nearly the same. Still another 50,000 were criminals. The servants and redemptioners were those who voluntarily exchanged labor and effort over some specific number of years of their lives (usually five to seven years or, in the case of children, generally until the age of twenty-five) for passage across the ocean to here. The criminals were guilty of everything from the most petty crimes to rape and murder and, when not so ordered, often were permitted to choose between being sent to these colonies (viewed by many as surely punishment enough for most crimes), or being sentenced to hang or spend agonizing years in an English prison. Be they servants or criminals, do not be ashamed of or embarrassed by such folks. They did something right; after all, you are the result.

There are many lists and reference works dealing with those groups of immigrants, all of which lists must be checked, since today those servants and criminals have millions of descendants. Caution: Most of those disadvantaged early people did not here accumulate real estate nor wealth during their lifetimes, so do not presume that an early ancestor was not in a certain place simply because his or her name does not appear in the land and existing tax records for that area.

Also, keep in mind that if the children of an early ancestor were known to have lived in a certain place, the chances are good that the parents previously also were there; some generations did not move. Remember; for the most part, the vast migrations west of the Appalachians did not get underway until the post-Revolutionary period, 180 years after the first settlement at Jamestown in Virginia.

Passenger Lists

Before you know it, through your efforts and the assistance and past work of others, you will have traced at least one line of your family to that point at which they no longer may be found in the American records. When that happens, remember that all who came here came by ship; there was NO other way.

You will find published many lists of ships' passengers—servants and the other categories, as well—who came to this or that province or colony. Within those lists often will be found the country of origin, and thereby you will find yourself contemplating a search in the "old countries." While that extended effort is outside the scope of this work, as you encounter ancestors' names in the records of those journeys and lists of travelers, remember to make careful notes for use later. Remember also that knowing WHEN an ancestor arrived here, or WHEN you lost track of him or her, will later be very important in picking up the trail in that foreign country of origin.

Keep in mind too that the passenger lists found in our libraries are far from complete. In fact, the present lists contain but three million or so immigrants, yet more than twenty one million came. Since all except the American Indians came by ship, if you do not find an ancestor in the now available lists, it probably is because the record is lost or has not yet been abstracted. So, later and over the years you will want to check new passenger lists whenever and wherever such become available. Notice too, many passenger lists are now available on the Internet, thanks to a determined effort by many to permit easy and free access to these very valuable sources.

Looking Abroad

When you reach that point in the past at which a family line may no longer be found in our records, you will fully know the value of your early notes as to the origins of surnames, and you will want to research in those countries. It is likely that you will find English, German, Irish, Scotch, Dutch, Italian and French names in your ancestry. Remember though that virtually every other nationality is somewhere represented in this great and proud nation.

Due to the ever-changing conditions in their native countries, many nationalities came here during rather specific periods. For example, "McCart" is Scottish, hence, knowing that fact, at some point in time you must look toward Scotland to pick up the trail. Indeed, a Scottish or an Irish surname may reveal to you that line of your family which was a part of the "Scotch-Irish" immigration of the eighteenth century (1700s). During that period many Scottish folks—their ancestors having emigrated first to Ireland, especially to the area of Ulster—will be found moving on to the Americas. It also may be important to your search to remember that even after that long voyage with its attendant hardships, the Scotch-Irish were noted for their inclinations to pick up their belongings and move to new territory.

Then too, your Irish ancestors may have come over in the middle of the last century, during and just after the Potato Famine, 1845-1860, a period of very difficult times in Ireland. Finally, many tens of thousands of Germans came, commencing in 1709. In fact, after the English, the Germans were the most numerous of our immigrant ancestors. So always make good notes about and use surnames as the valuable clues they are.

Using Library Catalogs

The catalog section of the library has been often mentioned. What is it and how is it used? Simply stated, a catalog (whether on computer or still in the old card system) is a quite complete index to the titles, authors, and subject matter to be found in that library. To use a catalog, first, look up your surnames, in case there is a written history for any of your family lines (such as the McCarts in our example). Then too, surnames often have been extracted from books in that collection and placed in alphabetical order in a specific or separate section of the catalog, just as were the family histories written over the years.

Look in the catalog under the county name ("Smith County" in the case of your imaginary grandmother Grace) to see if there are histories of the county which you have not examined. The library may have a map collection. If so, such usually are very helpful, so look in the catalog under "Maps, Smith County" and examine these. Be sure to check for titles or works under "River Township" in which Grace's family was shown by the census to have lived. Check under "veterans" for materials concerning local family members and societies. Local libraries often will have in their catalogs lists of area marriages, burials in local cemeteries, summaries of tax records, lists of former officials and office holders, church records, and many other local materials, much of which will be found on the family history shelves, with the balance in the *stacks*. By that time, you will have a feel for the locale, and you should be able to continue in the catalog search.

Ask the librarian if the stacks are "open" or "closed." Books in closed stacks must be specifically requested of the librarian, usually through the use of a *call slip* filled in with the *call numbers* you found in the catalog. The call numbers will be quite apparent on the computer screen (or are usually in the upper left hand corner of the card, if the old system of cards is still being used). If the stacks are "open," once you find the number, you simply go to the bookshelves and find it. As always, ask the librarian for help if you need it.

In virtually every library, in addition to the books, newspapers, and censuses mentioned, there are many additional records preserved on *microfilm* or *microfiche*. Microfilm and microfiche are photographic copies of source materials, and are indexed and cataloged in the same manner as if they were printed. Quite usually, the library will have a list showing the categories of such materials available, and will have easy-to-use film readers, which are the machines used for viewing microfilm and microfiche. If the library has a "reader-copier" you will be able to make a copy of any discoveries you make on these films.

In addition to the films and books owned by the local facility, thousands of others are available through rental services and *inter-library loan.* For a modest fee, the librarian will procure such other records for you to examine at your leisure. This feature is most important, since it opens up to you the collections of many of the great libraries of the world. Through its use, even in a small library you will be able to do extensive family research.

Note also that any branch of the Church of Jesus Christ of Latter Day Saints (the Mormons, previously mentioned) either will have research facilities for or will provide information as to another nearby Mormon church that does have such materials available. Such *Family History Centers*, as they are called, provide access to the vast resources of their organization and the library in Salt Lake City. You need but make contact with the local church through the phone directory, and there inquire after the facilities, hours, and services available in your area. Remember also, the addresses and times of operations of Family History Centers quite often can be found on the Internet, as well as information about ordering and using the films in their collection.

The Mormons are most helpful, and their resources are incredibly vast. Remember however, that even though they have tens of thousands of original documents and thousands of books, as with all libraries, a large part of their collection is made up of the writings of those who are untrained. So again, as with all derivative sources, the sources there found are only as good as were the authors of those writings. Still though, their family history library is the largest of all in this country and probably in the world, and you should make full use of this fine resource.

By this time, it should be apparent that good library research commences long before you leave home. And well it should; after all, if you are willing to spend the time, effort, and money to make the trip to a library, even if the distance is but a couple of miles, surely it is worth an hour or so of organizational effort prior to leaving the house.

As mentioned earlier, you will not be able to accomplish all of your objectives in one visit. So, select the names of two or three ancestors whose records you are likely to find in the library to be visited. Make a determination as to what categories of records you there intend to exhaust (marriage, death, birth, military service, church records, newspapers, county histories, property maps, estate records, deed and court abstracts, etc.). Then determine those years within which you must search for specific records for those persons. For example, for the years during which an ancestor was between fifteen and thirty-five years old, you will seek a marriage record; for the same fifteen to thirty-five year period prior to a marriage you will seek the birth record; and you will search for the records of those wars fought during the years when an ancestor was of the age group likely to have been involved (between fifteen and fifty for wars up to and including the Civil War, and between about eighteen and forty or so for the wars since then).

You will become sophisticated at the process of planning library visits sooner than you suspect. Remember the simple rule: 1) Write down the ancestors' names to be researched; 2) determine the type or categories of records to be searched for each; and 3) establish the span of years over which you will search within those particular records. Thus, "Names, Records, and Years" before you leave home, and then, until you have finished that effort, resist the temptation to wander to other records or family lines.

Make no mistake; your planning and diligence will be noticed by the librarians, and you soon will be readily distinguishable from those who do no planning before arrival. The first time a librarian taps you on the shoulder and asks if you are the researcher seeking such and such family lines, you will know you have arrived; a bona-fide researcher, and having fun.

Migration Routes

The movements of settlers have been previously mentioned, and it is important that you be aware of some of the routes and reasons by and for which your ancestors ended up in certain places. Generally speaking, the routes used in the long journey west and southwest followed age-old Indian trails and animal paths, which in turn were dictated by land barriers and waterways. Migrations and the westward movement are as much a part of the American personality as is our language, and knowledge of the roads, terrain, and rivers is vital to an understanding of that most interesting part of our heritage.

The reasons (and there were many) for which people went south and west often provide valuable clues in the search for ancestors. As the population grew in any area, the price of land increased and the availability decreased. After but a few decades of farming the soil was depleted, jobs became scarce, and restlessness overtook some. The population increased with the birth of children and the arrival of new immigrants who also sought work and new land, and whose presence served to compound the problems. Families grew up, and the younger members had no land to farm even if they were so inclined. Some fled the law and their own past and, incidentally, sometimes took new names, thereby creating "dead ends" for their descendant/researchers of today. Some, such as the Scotch-Irish already mentioned, came with a history of wanderlust; "itchy feet," as it was called.

For those and many other reasons, great pressure was exerted upon Eastern folks who were not firmly settled to move northwest, west, and south into the more sparsely settled frontier territories. As an example of how such migration patterns may be helpful, consider that in the eighteenth century (1700s), the Pennsylvania Dutch especially ("Dutch" as in "Deutsch," not as in Holland; the Germanic people), and others as well, moved from eastern Pennsylvania down the Great Philadelphia Wagon Road (now parallel to I-81) through the Shenandoah Valley to the central and western Carolinas, there to join the Virginians and others who also were moving south and west.

The next generation or so then moved west through Cumberland Gap and across the Wilderness Road, thence northwest to Kentucky, Ohio, Indiana and Illinois, or southwest across the Walton Road to Nashville, Memphis and beyond. At about the same period, many Easterners (again, the "Dutch" and others), either overland or up the St. Lawrence River and then through the Great Lakes, made the long journey to the western counties of New York and Pennsylvania or to northern Ohio, Wisconsin, and Michigan. Many of these New Englanders also went to Pittsburgh, and from there floated down the Ohio River to that same country to which their long-missing Yankee cousins had gone via the Carolinas and Kentucky.

Nearly all libraries can and will direct you to reading materials concerning the many routes used in such westward movements. If someday you are at a dead end and all else has failed, as a result of the dominant migration patterns you very well may be able to pick up the trail by searching to the east and northeast from the last known location of the ancestor.

Summary

So, our libraries are the place to look for family histories, censuses, abstracts, extracts, compilations, microfilm, newspapers, and the myriad genealogical writings of others. However for most of the original records of any county or area, you must visit the courthouses.

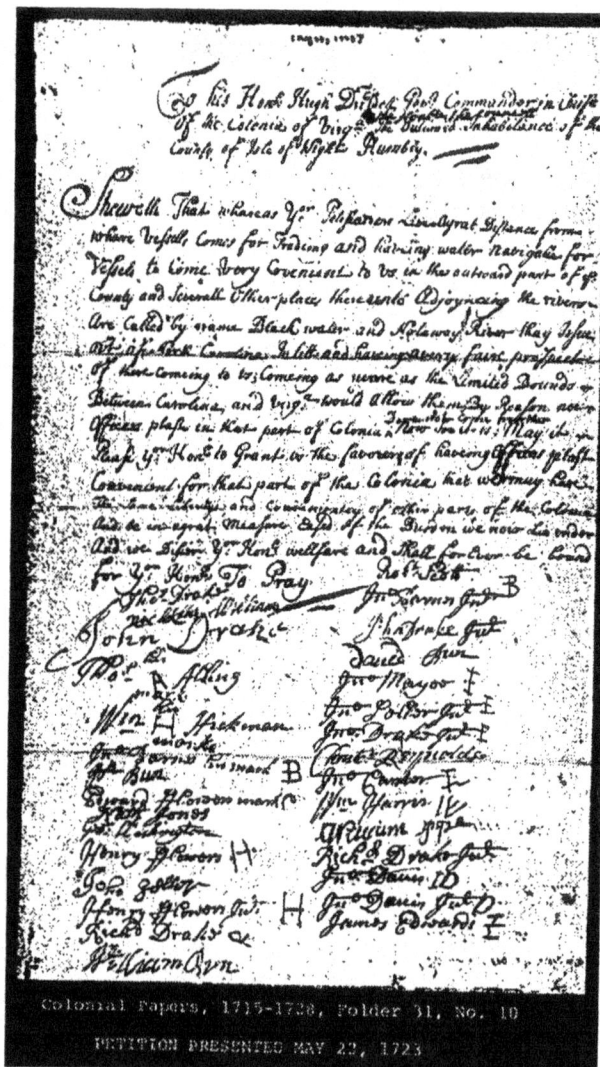

From the Virginia State Library and Archives; a copy of a 1723 petition of citizens of southern Virginia, who sought to induce the Royal Governor to move the customs house up the river and closer to where they lived. Because it reveals who resided in that immediate area (and who was literate) it is very valuable to the researcher.

5

Courthouses

As are the archives of the states and our nation, courthouses are collections of archival materials, and unlike libraries, which contain mostly *abstracts, extracts, summaries,* and comments derived from and concerning original records, the courthouses and the other governmental offices are places of original or near original records and writings from times past. Such documents and mementos make up a large portion of the total materials from which we trace our roots and upon which our governments at all levels are founded. Further, although we usually do not think of them as archives, national parks, shrines, historical sites, battlefields, and departments of government quite often have some of the documentary and historical materials and mementos that have to do with the origins of their peculiar aspect of government or history.

Just as the American collections in substantial part are housed in the places mentioned and the records of counties are in the local courthouses and offices, the collection of original letters, documents, photos, and the family Bible to be found among your own belongings comprise your family archives and are equally valuable sources of historical materials, at least to you and your extended family. Since most of the records found in family collections have not yet been the subjects of publication by genealogists, no references to these materials usually will be found in the libraries.

In addition to being of patriotic and historical value, such archival collections of records and artifacts remain almost unchanged since originally written or produced and thus represent the closest approach we have to the thoughts and ideas there found. These serve as the most reliable of the materials with which we can do research. We can come no closer to the truth of what occurred than through use of such original and near original records. (We say "near original" since a large portion of the early records are copies of still earlier ones which are now gone forever, especially in courthouses.)

While many of the early documents and source materials are carefully preserved, often guarded, and may be used only with great care, most are available to you for examination and study. As noted in the section concerned with libraries, those that are not open to general use often have been copied photographically—photos, microfilm, and microfiche—and one day will be in a format that may be accessed by computer. When such old records are physically open to the public, the keepers and custodians of these materials usually have rules concerning use, which rules will be explained to you upon your first visit there. You must abide by them.

In large part the records found in our courthouses contain the original source materials having to do with the local government and its citizenry. Land, tax, death, and court records concerning the rich and the poor alike were kept so that law and order could be maintained, taxes collected, and that title to property could pass from one person or generation to another with a minimum of difficulty. Unless a courthouse was burned or the records otherwise destroyed (and many were), most of those materials still exist for your pleasure and use. As examples, just as the Union armies destroyed much of Columbia and Richmond during the last days of the Civil War, the British burned Washington during the War of 1812. By those ruthless actions, countless records of the Confederacy, South Carolina, Virginia, and the federal government were destroyed and lost forever (including, incidentally, large portions of the Census of 1790 for Virginia).

So, while libraries for the most part (but not always) have only materials derived from earlier sources (the so-called "derivative sources") that save you both work and travel, you will want to view and gain copies of the original and complete documents, deeds, wills, artifacts, and those other records to which you have found references, as well as those that have not yet been abstracted. So it is that you must search in the archives and courthouses of all those jurisdictions where members of your family once lived.

Courthouse documents can be great fun. We know of one researcher who learned at a Virginia courthouse that one of his ancestors who died in 1698 had eight head of cattle, including a cow named "Madam"! A Kentucky resident who died in 1804 left to his daughter a cow named "Peggy, with a bell on her." In the 1679 inventory of the assets of our seventh-great grandmother, we found a recorder, two flutes, and an "hautboy" (oboe), all wind or reed musical instruments; a most unusual collection for that very early period.

Starting Courthouse Research

So, how do you approach the task of doing research in the local archives—the courthouses? As a general rule, unlike in the libraries, you may expect to find courthouse records organized in the order in which the events happened, that is, in *chronological* order, with alphabetical indexes covering specific time periods. So, the first rule is: before entering the courthouse fix firmly in your mind their names and that time period during which specific ancestors are thought to have lived within that county or jurisdiction. (Notice that federal courts have jurisdiction over areas which may or may not coincide with state lines.)

Stop and think back over your own life. Many records of your activities are in the courthouses where you have lived. To name but a few: your birth record (if issued locally), your driver's license; sometimes a record concerning your education or the schools you attended; your marriages; your military records and discharge; the documents showing the debts for your cars or furniture (*chattel mortgages*, financing statements, and other documentary materials required by the law when financing was done); the taxes and *assessments* levied on your properties by local government; your *real estate* purchases; any *mortgages* or *deeds of trust* on such properties; *liens* filed by or against you; lawsuits, divorces, and adoption proceedings in which you were involved; any *lunacy* records and criminal proceedings; public offices held; petit and

Typical of the documents that commenced, ended or are stored in local courthouses, here is a delightful 1904 "Marriage License" issued by Lunenburg County, Virginia. At the bottom appears the "return" of the officiating minister stating that he did indeed marry the couple pursuant to that license.

grand jury service performed; and someday your own death and estate records, to name but a few. Many, but not all, of these same records appear in some courthouse somewhere for most of your ancestors. Your task is to find which courthouses and to search the records therein.

A very large percentage of courthouse research involves property and the ownership of it. Indeed, records having to do with taxes, dispositions of the assets of dead people, and land are concerned with little else. Thus, you will benefit by remembering a few definitions for the words you may encounter. For our purposes here, your assets are everything you own of whatever nature and kind, and wherever located. Your liabilities are your total obligations to any person or institution, no matter of what nature those liabilities may be.

Of your assets, you doubtless own property of some sort or another. Property may be divided into two categories, a) *real property*, also called *realty* (real estate—land), and b) *personal property*, also called *personalty*. Personal property is easy to remember; it is everything you own other than land. Personal property may be divided into *tangibles* (automobiles, cattle, clothing, dishes, antiques, etc.) and *intangibles* (claims against others, *accounts receivable, corporate stock, bonds, promissory notes*, etc.).

So, having arrived at the county courthouse with a time period and an ancestor or two firmly in mind, how do you start? First, do not be intimidated or afraid of the surroundings. As Americans, we have been taught that our courts and courthouses are places of great solemnity, and that is as it should be. Nevertheless, most of the records of those who went before us are there for our careful use, so do not hesitate to jump in.

Maps

If you have not already gained a map of the area, here it really will be critical. Go first to the office of the *County Engineer* (he or she may be called the *County Surveyor*) or to the office of the *Tax Assessor;* one or the other should be able to supply a map of the county or perhaps a *quad* such as mentioned earlier. Also and often, an historical map or a map of landowners (reproductions of earlier maps of the county) will be available for minimal sums. If so, as suggested earlier, such maps are very helpful, since they often show, not only early landowners, but also communities that no longer exist, early roads, cemeteries and churches, old forts or Indian landmarks, fords and bridges, and other places of interest to you as a researcher. No matter which type may be available, remember that any map is better than no map, since if you have one at hand you will be able to spot the places to which references are made in the records being searched. As a result, such locations will be much more meaningful to you.

As is true of libraries, most courthouse materials are carefully indexed. Now, while the indexes found in one courthouse will be organized in very much the same manner as those found in every other courthouse, you will encounter minor variations. Always try to figure out the indexes for yourself, and if you can not, then, and only then, ask for help from the folks in charge. Almost always, they will help you. Even more so than with librarians, courthouse personnel have no interest in your family tales; they are working and have but little time to chat concerning ancestors. On an ever increasing basis, courthouse records are being computerized, and thus more readily usable than ever before.

Legal Terms

Legal documents and the words of lawyers are not difficult to read and understand, even though at first some of the words will be foreign to you. Words like *said, aforesaid, hereinafter, hereinbefore,* as well as the many Latin words and phrases formerly used, all were the products of the efforts by judges and lawyers to be precise in setting forth the rights and duties of the parties involved.

Even now, many old legal terms are still in use, and many still carry the Latin endings *-or* and *-ee*. Generally speaking, the -or ending (*suffix*) designates the person bringing about or performing the action described in the document, and the -ee suffix identifies the recipient or beneficiary of that effort or action. Thus, in deeds the seller or person transferring the property to another is called the *grantor,* and the buyer—the person receiving that property—is said to be a *grantee.* Likewise with a *mortgagor* and *mortgagee;* a *lienor* and a *lienee;* a *vendor* (seller) and *vendee* (buyer), etc.

Deeds

Deeds and most other records pertaining to land are found within the courthouses in the offices of the *Registers of Deeds.* The Registers' offices also may be called the offices of the *Clerk To The Court,* the offices of the *Registrar,* or by yet some other name. If none of those titles appears on the courthouse *directory* (usually found on a wall in the main hall) ask anyone working in any courthouse office where the deed records are, and they surely will point you in the right direction. As you consider deeds and related sources, remember that many locations on the Internet have transcribed documents that you may find at the courthouse. To remind you again, copies may have errors, so make note of the exact volume and page number no matter where found, and then you can write for copies and certified copies.

Most good researchers always order certified copies when asking for copies of any courthouse documents. By so doing, should you need such as proof for some organization of the future, there will be no question of the validity of what you have in hand and you won't have to return to that source to gain copies bearing a certification. Incidentally, certification means that the courthouse official who certified it is guaranteeing to the world that the copy you have is identical to the document of record.

Deeds and *instruments* for the transfer or sale of land are divided into several categories, and for our purposes, five types are of importance. They are the *mortgage deeds, deeds of trust, warranty deeds, quit-claims,* and *deeds of partition.*

Whether computerized or yet in the bound volumes, or both, in recent years the deed records, no matter of which of the above categories, have been indexed in two ways. One set of indexes is in the names of the grantors, called the *Grantor Index* or *Direct Index,* depending on which county and state you are in. Where still in bound volumes, usually located on the same shelf, or close at hand, will be found the other set of indexes alphabetized in the names of the Grantees. These volumes, in turn, are known as the *Grantee Index* or *Reverse Index.*

As many do, this researcher chose to have the Clerk to the Circuit Court of Sussex County, Virginia, certify this to be an exact copy of a document in the records there. It is remarkable for other reasons; it was actually signed by a group of men of the neighborhood who agreed that if William Hunt was allowed to build a grist mill, the damages to William Parker by the water which would back up from the new dam would be 10S. A fine keepsake by which to gain much insight into those lives of now 240 years ago.

Because of the extensive borrowing of money against land, especially during this century, a great number of mortgage deeds and deeds of trust have been recorded, as a result of which those categories of deeds are now in separate volumes and have their own indexes. Likewise, whether computerized or not, the mortgage records will be under the heading "mortgages." Remember though, such was not the case in the early days, when all deeds usually appeared in the same volumes and were indexed together.

Always remember that if an ancestor ever was a grantee (and so bought or received property), then later (whether voluntarily or not) when the property was sold or transferred away he or she also had to have then been a grantor. So, when you look under "McCart" in the Grantee Index and find a deed by which Grace's family bought property, you next need to look under the same name in the Grantor Index for the following years for the deed by which they later sold that same tract. By finding both documents, you not only will know when they moved from the property, but also may discover interesting facts previously not known to you.

Sometimes, yet fortunately not as often as some writers would suggest, deeds were not recorded, hence occasionally one of the two documents (the one by which they bought the land or the one by which they sold it) will not be found, and sometimes neither one. Instances in which deeds were not executed and recorded quite usually came about, not through oversight or neglect, but through an abandonment of the property or, more often, through the death of the owner. At death, of course, there was no one to sign the deed, and it really was unnecessary anyhow, since at the moment of death the land automatically went to whoever in the eyes of the law should rightfully have it. Note that where the ownership in land was lost for failure to pay taxes or through some other legal proceeding, quite usually there was a deed made in the name of that person as the grantor and was signed by a sheriff or other officer appointed by the court for that purpose.

Caution: For many of the very early records, there was but one index, and a transfer of property was often listed in that single index either by the grantor only or by both grantor and grantee. Remember; if only the grantors—sellers—are listed there, you only will find the deed by which your ancestor sold the property. However, that deed also may tell you from whom it was purchased by that ancestor. If so, take the name of the person listed there who sold the land to the ancestor, and search for that name in the earlier index volumes until you find the deed by which the property was deeded by that person to your ancestor. Do not forget that whenever you find an ancestor owning land there were two (2) deeds involved; the one by which the ancestor received the land and the other being the deed by which he or she transferred it to someone else. The only exceptions to that rule are when an owner died and the land passed through an estate; when that owner lost the land through failure to pay a mortgage; when it was taken for failure to pay taxes; or when he or she lost it as a result of a lawsuit.

Mortgages

Mortgages (*mortgage deeds*) transfer *title* in property from the borrower (*mortgagor*) to the lender (*mortgagee*). In mortgages (and deeds of trust, discussed below) the land serves as security for the loan made to the mortgagor, with the condition that when the money is paid back, the lender will *release* the mortgage; that is, cause the land rights to revert to the borrower. Since banks as we know them were uncommon (indeed, in the very early days, totally unknown), and since from the earliest times people have been willing to loan money to their kinfolk, early mortgages very often reveal family relationships previously unknown.

With mortgages, unlike deeds, your ancestor probably will appear only in the original mortgage signing his (or her) name as a mortgagor, since the release back to that borrower usually was (and still is) noted only on the margin of the original recorded mortgage deed. When such releases are found, carefully note the date, for (just as now) it may signify a move, a death, or perhaps a subsequent purchase of land by that same ancestor.

As noted, in the early days mortgages were generally recorded in the same volumes as all other deeds, so be careful and do not presume there was a sale or purchase of land by an ancestor until you read all of the words of the document. If it provides (and many different expressions may have been used to do so, most located near the end of the document) that upon the payment of a sum of money, the transfer (*conveyance*) will no longer be effective or valid, then that document is a mortgage and is not a deed. So, be careful to distinguish mortgages from deeds.

Computerized or not, mortgages are indexed in the same fashion as ordinary deeds—by mortgagor and mortgagee. So, simply search in the mortgagor indexes for the names of any ancestors who may have borrowed money and pledged their land as security. These fascinating documents should not be overlooked.

Deeds of trust (sometimes imprecisely called *mortgage deeds of trust*) are quite similar in purpose to mortgage deeds. However, in trust deeds, by reason of a past deep and abiding distrust of banks and moneyed people, the title to the real estate is transferred, rather than to the lender, to a third party who was agreed to by both the borrower and the lender and who, in turn, had an obligation to transfer the property to the lender if the debt was not paid or, instead, back to that borrower if the debt was paid as agreed. Remember that since in the early days, much more often than now, the parties and witnesses were relatives, the grantees in trust deeds, if not kin, usually were well known to or lived near the borrower or the lender, or to both. Again then, clues as to residency and kinship very often may be found in the names of the trustees and witnesses in such deeds.

So, if a mortgage or the debt set forth in a trust deed was not paid as agreed, just as now, the property went to the lender, thus revealing to you that these ancestors may have fallen upon hard times. Incidentally, hard times were not uncommon then. There was no social security, no welfare, nor were there any credit cards or food stamps. It is a fact, and we, like you, find it interesting that if our ancestors could not pay their bills, they sometimes were thrown into "debtors' prisons" and whether such debtors were at fault or victims of circumstance was scarcely considered. There, for sure, they would have no chance to work and pay debts.

Still though, Lady Justice followed their rules, just as with our rules she does today. So, do not find fault with your ancestors for such travails until you have learned why they suffered financial difficulties. Never make judgments nor apologies for, nor heap accolades on those who went before; what was, was.

Warranty Deeds

Most transfers of land to ordinary buyers were, and still are, accomplished by the use of *warranty deeds*. As the name suggests, such deeds convey land with warranties as to the quality and quantity of the ownership being transferred. By reason of the sanctity of ownership of land in the minds of particularly the English speaking peoples, and because of the importance to a buyer of proper title warranties and assurances that he was receiving everything for which he was paying, warranty deeds usually recite several facts.

Those facts are VERY important to you. They tell from whom the seller previously purchased or received the property, usually contain quite accurate descriptions of the boundaries of the land transferred and its size, and are specific in many other details. The *spouses* (wives or husbands) of both the seller and the buyer usually were named and the sellers' wives were always required to sign. So it is that warranty deeds often reveal clues, names, relationships, and property descriptions nowhere else to be found.

Marriages, Children, and Deaths

Deeds often state other interesting and genealogically very important facts. They often recite prior places of residence of the parties, e.g., "Silas Drake of the County of Lunenburg, Grantor." Since, even in the earliest days, a wife was required to sign her husband's deeds and thereby dispose of her *dower interests* (*inchoate rights*), the absence of such a spousal signature almost always reveals that either the ancestor had not yet married or that the wife had previously died. So, be alert to the absence of any mention of or the signature or mark of a spouse. If no spouse signed a deed conveying land, you are safe to presume at the time of the sale there was no such woman.

In the early days, perhaps more so than now, men and women needed each other to share in the never-ending, often brutalizing task of surviving. So it was that folks married, first, on the average, when the men were twenty-five or so and the women at twenty or thereabouts, and upon the death of their spouses, married again two, three, or more times. Since romantic love very often was not a prime consideration, re-marriages often took place within a few months or even weeks after the death of the mate. So, do not be shocked or entertain negative thoughts if your ancestor had a new husband or wife a month after the prior one died.

The absence of contraceptives in the early days resulted in children being born every twenty four to thirty-six months commencing at marriage and continuing throughout all the childbearing years of the woman. Incidentally, the childbearing years of women usually were over by about age forty-five. Then too, many women died during childbirth or shortly afterwards from sheer exhaustion or lack of medical care (and knowledge). About one out of every five children died during infancy or early childhood.

In fact, over a period of twenty-five years a wealthy sister of the Patriot George Mason bore ten children, only five of whom grew to adulthood. Thus, in analyzing a family, if the ancestor had five children who lived to adulthood, presume that at least one died as a child, for a total of six births. Then too, if you find a list of children in a census or otherwise whose ages were two or three years apart and there is a gap or break of three or four years between any two of the children, it is quite likely that either the wife died and the husband remarried during that interval, or that a child born during that interval died.

Notice that even though the near constant state of pregnancy was terribly difficult on some, if not all, the women of that day, the children, especially the males, provided much of the labor that was so necessary to expand the land and its harvest. Not only did they help with producing food for their families, but also in assisting in producing extra to sell, thereby providing added income with which needed "store-bought" goods might be purchased. The girl children were equally invaluable in helping with the day-to-day homemaking chores and by tending the youngest of the family members.

Quit-Claims

Back to deeds and another category of documents: *quit-claims*, often—though again, imprecisely—called "quit-claim deeds" (it can be argued that a quit-claim is not a deed at all, since it may convey no interest whatever and deeds always do). Unlike warranty deeds, quit-claims make no representations as to the adequacy, quality, or quantity of the sellers' title, and so have often been used by heirs to transfer their less than total interests to other heirs. As an example, suppose your father recently died *intestate* (without a will) and left as survivors your mother and four children (you and your three siblings). In most states, your mother would receive one third (1/3) of your father's property, and you four children would share equally in the remaining two thirds (2/3) of those assets.

As a result, you and each of your brothers and sisters would be entitled to one fourth of two thirds (1/4 of 2/3), or one sixth (1/6) of the value of the property. Then, if all parties—mother, brothers, and sisters—agreed that you should have the land, quit-claims naming you as grantee would be *executed* (signed) by your mother and each of the other three children, all acting as grantors. Those quit-claims, then, would transfer a total of five sixths (5/6) of the property to you and serve to reunite in you all the title. Remember, you already had the rights to one sixth when your father died. Notice that in such common cases there would be no deed from the father to anyone, since he died intestate while owning the land, and dead people don't write.

The genealogical value of quit-claims is that such instruments frequently recite the names of parents, of all of the known children, and sometimes even grandparents from whom the property or other assets might have originally come. It is very important to note, however, that occasionally, in the past and now, quit-claims have been executed by those who just might have an interest, yet in fact probably do not. Accordingly, do not presume that the execution of a quit-claim in and of itself establishes ownership, ancestry, or kinship. It always is wise to cross check the information learned from quit-claims by examining the determinations made by the court in the settling of the estate (the same will be discussed shortly).

A further caution: In the early days, as now, the laws concerning intestate death (death without a will) varied widely. Hence, if you seek to determine relationships or percentages of ownership where an intestate death has occurred, the law of the time period for that particular state or colony must be checked. Not only did the law vary, but in early times, by reason of the then prevailing law and *primogeniture*, first born

KNOW all Men by these PRESENTS, That we *John Walker & Robert Armstrong both of upper Pacton in the County of Lancaster and Robert Semple of the Town of Carlisle in the County of Cumberland & Province of Pennsylva. Yeomen*

are firmly held and bound unto the Honorable *RICHARD PENN*, Efq; Lieutenant Governor and Commander in Chief of the Province of *Pennfylvania*, and Counties of *New-Caftle, Kent*, and *Suffex*, on *Delaware*, in the Sum of *two* Hundred Pounds, good and lawful Money of *America*, to be paid to the faid *RICHARD PENN*, Efq; his certain Attorney, Executors, Adminiftrators, or Affigns; To the which Payment well and truly to be made, We bind ourfelves jointly and feverally, for and in the whole, our Heirs, Executors and Adminiftrators, firmly by thefe Prefents. Sealed with our Seals. Dated the *27th* Day of *September* in the Year of our Lord One Thoufand Seven Hundred and Seventy *three*

THE CONDITION of this OBLIGATION is fuch: That if there fhall not hereafter appear any lawful Let or Impediment, by Reafon of any *Pre-Contract, Confanguinity, Affinity,* or any other juft Caufe whatfoever; but that the above-mentioned *John Walker with Mary Gaskens of Northumberland County in The Province Aforeid Spinster*

may lawfully marry; and that there is not any Suit depending before any Judge Ecclefiaftical or Civil, for or concerning any fuch *Pre-Contract;* and alfo if the faid Parties, and each of them, are of the full Age of Twenty-one Years; and are not under the Tuition of his or her Parents, or have the full Confent of his or her Parents or Guardians refpectively to the faid Marriage; and if they, or either of them, are not indented Servants; and do and fhall fave harmlefs and keep indemnified the abovenamed *RICHARD PENN*, Efq; his Heirs, Executors, and Adminiftrators, for and concerning the Premifes; and fhall likewife fave harmlefs and keep indemnified the Clergyman, Minifter, or Perfon, who fhall join the faid Parties in Matrimony, for, or by Reafon of his fo doing; then this Obligation to be void, and of none Effect; or elfe to ftand and remain in full Force and Virtue.

Sealed and Delivered in the Prefence of

John Henry
John Agnew

John X Walker
Robt Armstrong
Robt Semple

From Pennsylvania; a very interesting bond posted by two men assuring Cumberland County that there were no legal impediments to the proposed marriage of John Walker and Mary Gaskens. A wonderful memento for their descendants, and one typically found in courthouses across the country.

sons very often received all assets owned by the father, with but an allowance (dower) or rights in the income from the property going to the widow for her lifetime. Such matters as the early laws almost always can be found in articles in the state genealogical or historical society journals.

As an interesting example of primogeniture, it is believed that when the wealthy William Huntt died intestate in Virginia in 1668, his first son William, Jr., received the entirety of his father's assets, less a maintenance allowance for life to the widow, Judith. Judith then was remarried to an affluent widower with sons. Next, Judith had a son by this new husband, and then that husband died—once again, intestate. Then Judith died intestate. The result, unfair as it may now seem, was that, despite all the wealth, the new son got nothing from any of the deaths since both fathers had earlier sons who inherited all of their assets, and the mother Judith, being a married woman, by law owned nothing, except for her personal property which went to her eldest son, William, Jr.

Deeds of Partition

The last category consists of *deeds of partition.* Sometimes as a result of differences among family members in their claims against an estate, or as a result of a lawsuit by one heir or joint owner against other heirs or joint owners, a court is called upon to make a physical or financial division of property, including a partition of the real estate. In such cases, if the court finds that to make such a division of the real estate it must determine the degree of kinship among the parties, then the deeds resulting from that court action—usually called deeds of partition—very often will name all of the heirs, and also the degree of the relationship of each to the other, or to the dead person, or to both.

Measures of relationships like these are called "degrees of *consanguinity*" if the relationship is "by blood," or "degrees of *affinity*" if the relationship is through marriage. Deeds of partition will be found in a) the deed records in the Register's (clerk's, etc.) office, indexed in both the grantor and grantee index volumes (or on their computer), b.) or in the courts' minutes (see below), or c.) in the courts files, usually found in the office of the *prothonotary* (clerk of the court), or in all three places. Such files of courts nearly always are indexed in the names of all of the parties to the lawsuit, hence are easy to seek out.

Consideration In Deeds

As to deeds in general, the money or other thing of value given or paid by the grantee to the grantor, called the *consideration,* often is very important to the researcher. When reading deeds, the consideration will be stated in the first part of the document and should be read very carefully. As in the Silas Drake deed illustration (though the words may vary slightly from place to place), the traditional phrase used to describe consideration is "...in consideration of the sum of $250.00, in hand paid, the receipt whereof is hereby acknowledged...." Note too, that since in the early days (and now as well) property often was transferred to relatives in consideration of "love and affection" or in exchange for care, those or similar words sometimes will appear in the consideration clause instead of an amount of money. So again, such statements reveal family relationships and also serve to add color and detail to the stories of the lives of our ancestors.

As mentioned in the section on libraries, until the Revolution the American colonies used English money; pounds (£), shillings (S or s), and pence (d or p). However, after our independence many Americans found the use of anything English to be repugnant, and so, until we had an established currency some years later, many merchants and the new states (former colonies) printed, circulated, and dealt in their own money. Occasionally too, Spanish and French currency were used (pieces of eight, francs, etc.). Further, *negotiable instruments* (bills of exchange, bills of lading, warehouse receipts—especially for tobacco, cotton, and grain, etc.—were circulated widely and used as money.

The result was that such "money" sometimes turned out to be worthless. In cases where the deeds revealed a type of currency that did turn out to be of no value, the sellers had the written proof needed to void the transactions. Thus, unless a property was paid for in silver or gold (and often even then), the type of money used was almost always spelled out.

Typical of deeds to be found in all courthouses, from Lunenburg County, Virginia, here is a copy of an 1888 deed by which "J. J. Walker and L. Walker, his wife" (grantors) sold to Silas J. Drake (grantee) 113 acres of land in that county. Silas paid $250.00 for it; about $10,000.00 in the money of today.

So what? Such monetary difficulties provide meaningful clues for the genealogist, since often the place from which the buyer came was revealed when the type of money was specified, e.g., Proclamation money (from North Carolina), Virginia money, New York gold coin, Current money of Pennsylvania, "Ten Pounds, Sterling" (English currency backed by silver) and "receipt for 4000 lbs of Virginia sweet tobacco and cask." So, by carefully reading the words describing deed consideration you may learn where an ancestor previously lived or did business.

Locating Real Estate

Deeds also describe the location of the property, sometimes in a most complete fashion and sometimes not quite so. Read these descriptions carefully, noting all landmarks, rivers, roads, and especially any names of neighboring landowners. As always, make careful notes. Better yet, have such documents copied and then visit the offices of the County Engineer (County Surveyor) or the Tax Assessor. If they have the time to spend with you (be sure to ask), inquire if there are enough boundary details given in that deed to permit you to locate the properties on their maps. Though, as in the Silas Drake deed shown, often no clues by way of landmarks are given, sometimes there will be sufficient information by which to find the property. If so, you will find it pleasant and most meaningful to drive out to land once owned by ancestors. You will learn much, and again family history will come to life. If you do, be sure to take photographs and always accurately plot the tract on your own maps.

If you are fortunate and locate an ancestral home property, you might walk up to the door and knock and introduce yourself. Remember though, you are on private property, so be prepared to be told to leave. Very often, however, the present owners are delighted to hear the history of their home and you may be invited inside. Then too, the present owners may know more than you do about your ancestors, and the conversation may provide the breakthrough you have been needing.

Probate Records

In that section of the courthouse wherein are found the *probate records*, much more is to be learned. In some places the courts that handle probate matters are called the *Surrogate Court*, or occasionally the *Orphans Court*, the *Common Pleas Court*, the *Superior Court*, the *Supreme Court*, or the *Circuit Court*. Still other names and courts are used and found in different places. If none of those titles appears on the courthouse directory, again ask anyone employed in any of the offices where you might find the probate or death records. They will know what you are talking about and will direct you to the right office.

Whatever the names used, these courts handle matters of death, mental or legal incompetence, orphans' or children's claims, and other matters wherein the physical and mental well-being of the citizenry requires the attention, action, or protection of the court. When you arrive at the probate division or section, ask where the indexes to wills and administrations are located.

As with the deed and mortgage records, you will find some variations in the records from place to place. If the index or the files themselves are computerized, all the years of records yet existing likely will be accessible from one place on the computer. If the index is yet in bound volumes, the records are usually divided into time periods, e.g., "Beginning to 1780", "1781 to 1940", etc., and within the computer index or in each of those volumes, almost always you will find the names of deceased ancestors, orphans, etc., who were the subjects of the courts' actions during that time period listed in alphabetical order. Then too, in most places, within the volumes the estates will be set forth in chronological order with an alphabetical index within that volume itself directing you to the appropriate page for the person sought. As always, if you do not understand the local indexing system after carefully examining it, ask someone there if they have the time to assist you.

Estates

In the estates volumes—again computerized or not—and usually following the names of dead persons (the *decedents*), will be found columns of notes that set forth, summarize, and date the activities in that decedent's estate, and a number or reference to a file that will contain the original papers and proceedings—in many places still called the *jacket*. After locating the ancestor in the index and there finding the estate file number, simply ask the folks working there where in the building those files are located, and then commence your examination of that particular numbered file.

In the case of original papers, sometimes the clerk or other person in charge will be reluctant to permit you to use them. When that happens, be polite yet persistent, and assure them that you will be very careful and not make marks in or remove items from that file (and then so conduct yourself). If the clerks in that office stand over you while you use the original files, do not be offended. It is likely that they do so with everybody because, unfortunately, too many researchers have stolen papers from their files.

It is very important to remember that if an ancestor owned land in two or more counties, you likely will find estate proceedings for him or her in each of those counties. So, if an ancestor was a person of some wealth or is known to have dealt in land, check the surrounding counties for additional estate files and deeds to and from that person. Such supplementary estate proceedings usually were (and still are) called "*ancillary* administrations." If the courthouse in the county in which your ancestor lived was burned sometime in the past, such ancillary proceedings and deeds recorded in neighboring counties sometimes are among the only sources for estate and land records for that ancestor.

Nearly all persons down to now have done business or been otherwise involved in *jurisdictions* (counties and towns) other than their home town or county. Accordingly, even if an ancestor was not affluent and the courthouse did not burn, it is good to spot check the records of surrounding counties. At least look at the deed and tax records there.

Testate Death Proceedings

Back to the decedents' estates files. In such files you usually will find numerous papers and writings. When a person dies, having previously executed a will, he or she is said to have died *testate* as opposed to *intestate*: remember both words! In a testate death it is the will that dictates who of the heirs shall get what. Immediately after death the witnesses who signed the will are summoned to court and are asked to *prove* the will, i.e., to prove through their *testimony* that the will filed there actually was signed and acknowledged by the decedent to be his or her will. Thereafter, the appointed *executor* (a man) or the *executrix* (a woman) *executes*—carries out—the provisions of the will and performs those duties required of him or her by law. After the funeral expenses and taxes, all debts must be paid and all receivables collected, and then a *final settlement* takes place dividing and distributing the remaining assets as directed by the dead person in that will.

The objectives of all such probate activity are to finally and positively conclude all of the earthly business of the dead person, and to see to it that all of his or her worldly possessions are properly distributed to his or her creditors, legal heirs, and beneficiaries. Having accomplished those objectives, the estate is then *closed* by the court. In every one of those activities, a written record is made that has value and provides clues to the researcher.

As with all other documents, very carefully examine all wills. Even more so than with deeds, the witnesses found there usually were friends, relatives, or neighbors. Incidentally, a person may die testate, yet not have executed a will. How so? If death is imminent and, being aware of that immediacy, the dying person makes a) positive statements disposing of his or her property, and b) these statements are written down shortly thereafter by those who heard them, the probate courts usually will give full legal effect to such last intentions and wishes. That written document is known as a *nuncupative* will and, as with other wills, the persons who witnessed such deathbed declarations almost always were friends, neighbors, or relatives. So it is that, once again, all names should be carefully noted. Notice too, that the dates of nuncupative wills will be very close to the date of death.

Finally as to the wills themselves, if a person left a list, written in his own hand, of his intentions and wishes concerning to whom his assets should go, even if that document fails to meet the strict requirements of law as to witnesses, acknowledgment, and form, it still is given great weight and consideration and is known as a *holographic* will. Since, unlike in early times, all of us now have ready access to lawyers, holographic wills were much more common in early times than they are now.

It is important that the researcher be aware that within the early courts records, even if the death date was not given (and often it was not), usually the dates will be found upon which the will was *executed*—signed—and the date upon which it was recorded. The date of recording is not the same as the date of death. Death took place between the date of the execution of the will and the recording date. Considering that early law (as now) required that the authorities be notified of a death at the very next *term* of court (when it next met), the actual date of death usually can be approximated by learning from the courts' records (of which below) the date upon which the preceding session (term) of court ended and the date the term in which the estate was commenced began. (Courts usually were held every three months and so often were called *quarter sessions*; they lasted from a few days to several weeks, depending upon how much business the court had to accomplish.)

So, if you find that an ancestor's will was recorded on the 10th of May, 1765, and you then learn from the courts' minutes that the prior term ended on April 15th of that same year, almost surely the ancestor died between those dates. Since early newspapers seldom noted the deaths of other than famous and rich folks, very often this simple calculation is the only means by which to arrive at an approximate death date. Do remember, however, that where the weather usually prohibited movement—as in New England in January—courts were lenient in enforcement of the requirement that the death be reported at the very next term. So be careful in your estimates if the recording took place in winter months; in February or March, for example.

Intestate Death Proceedings

As noted, if a person died without a will he or she universally is said to have died intestate, and an *administrator* (man) or an *administratrix* (woman) is appointed by the court to perform the same tasks as did the executor or executrix who were appointed in the will and testate death examples set out above; in both cases, under the direct supervision and control of the probate court. Where a death is intestate, the laws of *descent and distribution* established by the state in which the dead person made his home (was *domiciled*) take the place of the provisions (*devises* and *bequests*) in the will in testate deaths and direct to whom the assets of the decedent should go. Such laws are said to control *intestate succession.*

Bonds, Inventories, Appraisements, and Sales

In all estate proceedings, whether testate or intestate (unless the dead person through a provision of the will or by the probate court specifically waiving the requirement), a *bond* must be posted. This bond must be sufficient in amount to guarantee the court and the heirs that the executor or the administrator, as the case may be, will see to it that the burial is accomplished and paid for, that the taxes are settled, that all other debts are paid and the receivables collected, that the assets of the dead person are protected from waste and distributed as required, and that the estate is closed. Such bonds are in an amount of money set by the court and are valuable to genealogists for two reasons. First, they usually were (and still are) about twice what the court thought the assets of the dead person were worth, thus reflecting wealth or the lack of it, and, secondly, the people posting that bond or acting as *sureties* were named. Those named sureties are important because, as with witnesses to wills and deeds, nearly always the persons posting bonds or acting as sureties were known or related to the families of the dead persons; there were but VERY few professional bondsmen then.

In addition to the will and bond, of particular interest is the *inventory* (sometimes called *inventory and appraisement*) of the assets of the dead person. The inventory is a list of every asset (and its value) known to have belonged to the dead person at the moment of death. By carefully studying that document a vivid picture of the farm or the house and furnishings may be drawn, from which one may reconstruct many of the daily activities of the family. After visiting the site of the farm of an early ancestor, one artist and researcher was able to reconstruct and then paint a remarkable likeness of the long decayed and abandoned farm, from just the remains of the foundations of buildings and the inventory of the assets found in the estate papers. What fun!

Typical of an early estate from Sussex County, Virginia, here is a copy of the inventory and appraisal of the 1760s estate of Thomas Oliver. Notice that the names and values placed on his slaves are noted, just above the horses and the cattle! An incredibly interesting document for his descendants, and others as well.

If there was a public sale or auction of the furniture or other property (in the early days, called *outcry* or *sale by outcry*), that fact will appear in the file in the form of a list of goods sold, very often with the names of the buyers. Quite usually again, relatives will appear there and so reveal something of their whereabouts at the time. Such sales also reveal much about values of merchandise during that period, and once again the lives of your ancestors become more real.

Another document often found in the estate papers, usually called the *summary of debts and accounts*, reveals relationships with others previously unknown. Frequently one of the most difficult facts to ascertain is the occupation (if other than farmer) of an early ancestor. In addition to the inventory, summaries of accounts often provide clues as to those means of livelihood by naming suppliers of materials, merchants, or buyers of products.

Especially in intestate deaths, the *final order* of the court that distributes the assets will name all of the children or, if none, the *next of kin*. Incidentally, the expression next of kin refers to all relatives other than parents and children. Where a child has previously died and his or her children are to receive what would have been his or her share of an estate, those children also will be named and are said to take their share *per stirpes* (Latin).

In summary, by learning where an ancestor died and examining all of his or her estate records, kinship and many interesting facts from the life of that ancestor will be learned. In addition to the names of the spouse and children, you may find the precise location where death took place ("drowned in the Blackwater," "killed by a train while crossing Driskill Pike," etc.), or the cause of death may be stated ("blood poisoning," "struck by lightning," etc.), or the age of the dead person as positively established by the court, perhaps the names of slaves or a complete list of land holdings, furniture, and other personal property owned, lists of accounts receivable and of debts, the names of neighbors and friends, and much, much more.

Lawsuits and Other Court Activities

In addition to the land and probate records, over the centuries many other legal activities were recorded. Since time immemorial, our courts have been called upon to formally deal with the everyday problems and conflicts by the process called *litigation* (the determinations of differences between people through the use of law and its processes). Moreover, over those same centuries our desire for continuity and an ordered society has demanded that written records be kept of the rulings of courts acting in such conflicts. Many of these records have been preserved and are of very great value to you.

As the early judges, justices of the peace, magistrates, mayors, and chancellors sat hearing civil, criminal, and probate cases, they or their clerks (or both) usually entered the rulings and final decisions made into notebooks. Further, during the course of the proceedings the judges themselves often made notes and entered rulings as to evidence, etc.

Those rulings were entered in volumes called variously *courts' minutes, courts' journals, order books,* or *courts' orders*. Note that the words used to describe those entries and notations varied widely, and any given volume may have final decisions, entries, notes, doodling, comments about evidence presented, notes as to some future event, and even the weather. Except for the recordings and transcripts by stenographers and tape recordings, there no longer are permanent records kept of the notes made by judges during trials, so the differences between minutes, orders, journals, and entries have disappeared. Perhaps less than half of the existing genealogical source materials have been the subject of abstract and extract work, and courts' minutes, journals, and order books surely rank prominently among the records yet to be studied.

When indexed, courts' writings were set out in the names of the parties as they appeared on the case caption. Most often, however, early minutes and journals were not indexed and remain only in chronological order in decaying volumes. So, since nearly all families were at one time or another involved in litigation, even if only as witnesses or jurors for coroners', grand, or petit juries, or as members of inquests, it is necessary to search through those orders and minutes for the whole period of time during which an ancestor is known to have been within that county or jurisdiction. Start with those volumes covering months or years thought to include important events in the life of the ancestor. For example, if you know that an ancestor was born about 1740 and from the deed records that he first appeared buying land in 1775, it is reasonable to assume that he might appear thereafter for a considerable number of years, but not likely that he will appear much before since he was but a young man and probably had but few assets.

Reading Early English

The search through courts' records often is not an easy one, for even after *Elizabethan* style written English (so called because of the influence of Queen Elizabeth I of England) fell into disuse during the eighteenth century (1700s), the quill pen handwriting of the early judges and clerks often was nearly illegible. Further, the readability of those entries has not been improved by the passage of the centuries or by the poor quality ink then available in the colonies. Nevertheless, such records surely are worth the effort required to read them, and many provide real insight into the times during which your people lived, struggled and died.

With a little practice you will be able to read early written English. Start with an extra copy of an early document so that you may make marks and notes on it, then go through the document very carefully and circle those words and letters which you do recognize. You will find that some of the letters will not be familiar to you, some examples of which are the longhand, lower case letter "s" which often was written like the letter "f" - ∫ ; "ss", as in the name Jesse, might be written as "Jeppe" 𝓙𝓮𝓹𝓹𝓮 , "Jefse" 𝓙𝓮𝓯𝓼𝓮 , or "Jeffe" - 𝓙𝓮𝓯𝓯𝓮 ; "e" which often appeared like the letter "o" -𝓸 ; and "d" which was commonly written like the number "6" backwards - 𝓭 . The word "and" often appeared as a simple loop - ᴈ ; "th" quite often was written quite like the letter "y" (called a thorn) - ᵧ; and "s" with a "d" loop over it -ᶳ - very often was used for the word "said". Finally watch out for the symbol (usually called a crossed p) which appears like a complex letter "p" - ℘ ,it often meaning variously "pre-" or "per-".

Frequently, common words were abbreviated (even in legal documents) by writing enough of the letters to make the word recognizable and then, over the top of those letters, placing the last or near last letter. "Alex" with "r" above for the name Alexander - *Alex̄* , and "Rich" with the "d" over for Richard - *Rich* , are but two examples. Often, even in the early twentieth century, indistinguishable flourishes were given to signatures, to the first letter of the first word, and to the last letter in the last word of a sentence or paragraph - / ⟩ . In working through a document, try to ignore such marks and decorations.

Typical of documents we all must undertake to read, here is a difficult example. From the Virginia Archives, shown is a copy of a portion of the will of Owen Griffith who died in 1698. Though written in the near-Elizabethan English of their day, it is readable with but some effort, and surely is worth the exertion to Owen's descendants.

By the time you finish the first reading you will have recognized many of the letters and words. Then go back and start over again, and stay with it until the meaning of the document becomes clear to you. Each re-reading will bring greater understanding, so be persistent.

Loose Papers

Often in the courthouses will be found groups of what are usually known as "loose papers." These are the miscellaneous pleadings (legal statements submitted by lawyers to courts), exhibits, documents and memoranda which were a part of the early lawsuits or simply were left at the courthouse. As now, such papers usually were not thrown away, lest they should later prove to be needed by someone, yet often were stored in a quite haphazard manner. Loose papers usually are open to the public, however, as the name suggests, they are unbound and generally have no particular order or index. Still, the time spent looking through such loose materials will be amply rewarded if you come across an ancestor's signature, lawsuit, receipt, or affidavit.

Likewise, to be found in all courthouses are some record books which over the years have been kept on a shelf of miscellaneous materials. There, often you will find a surveyor's notebook, a school board ledger, minutes of county commissioner's meetings, health records, meetings of school boards, and no telling what else. Examine these materials, and if any fall within the time period in which you are searching look through them thoroughly. Your family well may be there; somebody's ancestors are!

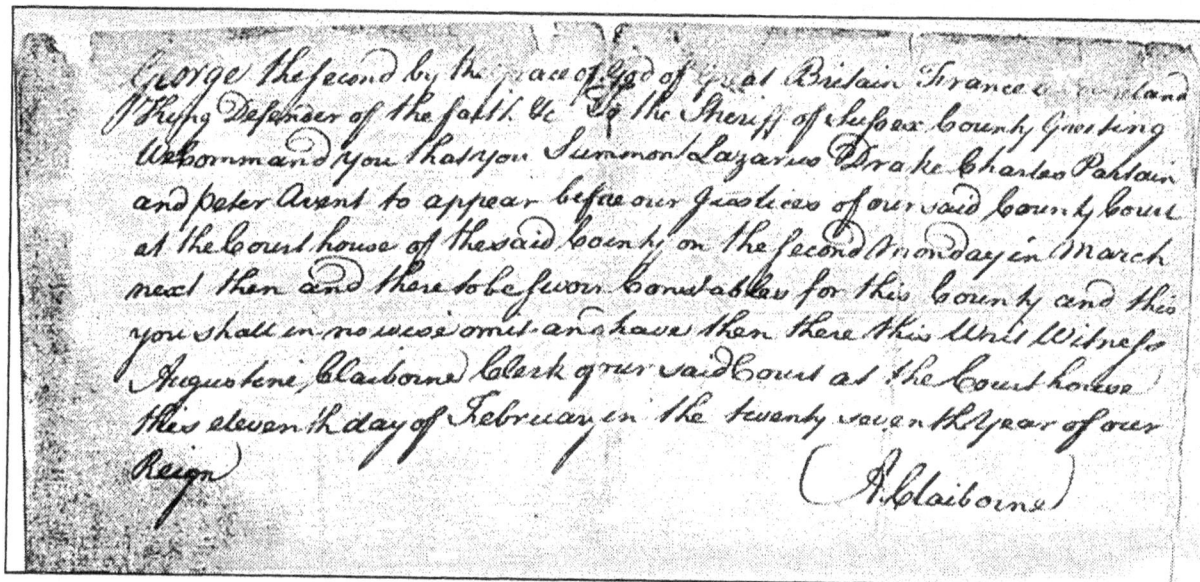

Here, from the "Loose Papers" of Surry County Virginia, is one of the millions of exciting discoveries awaiting those who are diligent. From the 1755 records of that county, it is stated that, in the name of our King George II, citizens Lazarus Drake, Charles Partain, and Peter Avent were sworn in as Constables for their districts.

Similarly, early clerks and registrars of deeds often were not sure where a particular document should be filed or recorded, yet knew that such materials should be preserved. In those instances, such papers were often filed in the *Miscellaneous Records* and have a separate index aptly called the *Miscellaneous Index* which will list the involved parties in alphabetical order. Always check it carefully for the time periods of your ancestors.

Naturalization Records

As we have seen, until we became a nation at the close of the American Revolution most of our people considered themselves to be, and indeed were, English men and women. At the close of the American Revolution almost all those who lived here were declared to be citizens, however most who came after were not.

So it was that it became important to our government that new arrivals become Americans. The process of becoming a citizen was and still is known as *naturalization.* Both one's *Intent To Be Naturalized* and the naturalization itself were supposed to be filed and accomplished within the jurisdiction in which the new citizen (or citizen-to-be) lived, thereby providing the local civil, criminal, and taxing authorities with knowledge of that immigrant's presence.

Accordingly, you may find the naturalization of an ancestor in the records of either the local courts, or in those of the federal court system, or both, or neither. If the indexes do not reveal a naturalization for an ancestor who you believe surely was there, ask the local court clerk for help in locating such records. They will tell you whether the same are likely to be found within their records, or direct you to that Federal courthouse where you may find them. At times, such records will be found locally in the Miscellaneous Index or even in the deed records, and in those seaport cities through which many immigrants came the Clerks of the Courts sometimes have created rather complete indexes of such people.

Be aware that naturalization records usually contain only non-specific references to an area of origin, the person's name, and the date he or she was naturalized (or filed an Intent to be Naturalized). Naturalization records quite usually do not contain birth dates nor the names of parents, spouses, or children, nor will you usually find the names of the ships by which they came here.

Mention was made of the federal court system. Their records are nearly identical in form to those kept by the states' courts, however are wholly different as to the content (activities, litigation and participants), and they maintain almost no records concerning local government and no deed or mortgage records. So what may be found there? Their records of lawsuits (including those involving income taxes), criminal activities, and federal juries, both grand and petit, are superb. Simply go to the local U.S. Post Office and inquire where the federal courthouse is for your area of search; there are two or more for most states and at least one in every state.

Tax Records

Lastly, yet surely not least, are the tax records to be found in every courthouse, state or federal. These are extremely valuable sources, since they reflect ownership of assets (and wealth or a lack of it). Since the earliest times, governments have tithed, taxed, sought to tax, or exempted from taxation the assets of all citizens who could be identified or located. Hence, even if an ancestor owned no real estate, he or she may have—and probably did—own some personal property (a cow or a horse, perhaps) upon which a tax was assessed or at least considered. So it is that such people likely will be found in a tax record someplace. Moreover, as to the very poor, the personal property tax lists (*tax rolls*) may be the only records to be found. Indeed, if an ancestor owned or

Tithables were citizens who were eligible to be taxed, and here is a list of such people taken by Constable Lazarus Drake in 1755. From the "Loose Papers" of Surry County, Virginia, here is his handwritten list. It is a wonderful listing of who lived as neighbors, how many tithables were in each household, and the names by which those men were known to all. A truly great find for the descendants of all named.

leased no real estate, or lived out on the edge of settlement, there may not have been even an administration of his or her estate, and so no record of that life or death may appear except that which may be found in the tax books.

When searching tax records, remember that the terms "personal property" and "personalty" both refer to that group of assets which consists of all property other than real estate. Personal property taxes usually were assessed on an annual basis and were levied against all men who were of age (as seen, not necessarily eighteen or twenty-one years old) and all women who were widows or single and had assets (sometimes called by the French *femme sole* or *femme sole trader*).

Since such levies were annual, one often may trace an ancestor over a considerable number of years, and just as when that person no longer appears you may presume he or she either died or moved away, you may presume that during those years before a first appearance he or she either was not of age or had not yet arrived at that place. Thus, you will have gained knowledge of yet more events in the life of an ancestor.

Remember that the early enumerations of tithables also were tax lists, the word *tithe* having come from ancient English law and its requirements that increase from the land—crops, etc.—and the fruits of one's labors might be assessed for tax purposes. So too were *polls* (that term simply meaning lists of persons by count), and a poll tax sometimes was called a *head tax* since it was levied against all who were in a particular class or group of people. Incidentally, of all levies the poll taxes were the most despised, especially by the poor or nearly so, since, unless specifically excluded, these taxes often were levied against all, even infants, old widows, and the disabled or infirm, without regard to their ability to pay.

Those who were considered *tithable*—required to pay a tax—varied from time to time, however generally it may be said that males over sixteen, all slaves, and all free blacks or other free persons of color fell within these categories, and that women (again, unless femme sole) were not tithable. Notice that if an ancestor is found with three tithables shown within his household (three persons chargeable to him for tax purposes), you have no clues as to the number of females within the household. To approximate the number of women and girls in the house, since their numbers usually were about equal to the numbers of men plus the live-ins (men did not live as long as women), simply double the number of tithables listed other than the slaves.

Most importantly, tax lists reveal the presence of an ancestor in a certain geographical area or jurisdiction, and tell you something of his or her belongings and household wealth. Caution: the numbers designating the unnamed tithables or those subject to the poll taxes that are listed with the names of ancestors again may be misleading, since, as we have learned, there may be apprentices and others for whom an ancestor was taxable yet who were not immediate family. Thus, it should not be presumed that unnamed yet taxed persons were kin to the head of household.

Very early local tax records, if they have not been removed to a local library, historical society, or the states' archives (or to the trash dump!), usually will be found in the Clerks of Courts offices, with the deed records, or in the offices of the county Tax Assessors. If you do not find them, ask at the Assessor's office; they will know where they are, if they still exist.

Nearly always, as with deeds, tax record indexes are divided into time periods, and then within each time period the taxpayers will be set forth in alphabetical order. With these records, as with all others, if you can not locate the index on the computer or among the materials or, when found, can not figure out how to use it, ask someone in that office. They will help, so utilize these fine sources.

Good Genealogy Manners

A word should be said concerning conduct in libraries and courthouses. In all your activities you should both exercise and encourage others to use good genealogy manners. Too many folks are noisy, inconsiderate, and demanding while researching. Especially in the courthouses, most of the others working there and with those records are at the task of earning a livelihood, and so we should work quietly, without family chatter, and seek to learn in advance of those times and days during which the schedules are particularly tedious. Simply call ahead and inquire as to rules, if any, and of the times which are the most convenient to that office to have you there. You will be amazed at how much better you will be treated and how much more help will be available to you by reason of that small courtesy on your part.

Care of Records

The folks at the courthouse are custodians of archives which often are very fragile and old. One of their responsibilities is to care for and preserve such materials. As researchers we too have an obligation to act in such a fashion that future generations may enjoy our hobby. Too often, family researchers, having learned that such records are public, have been abusive and failed to exercise care in handling the old books and documents. Never tear or make marks in books and records and, unless the rule directs you to not re-shelve books, always put them back exactly where you found them.

If you find that someone before you has attempted to "correct" an entry in a public record, be skeptical; the correction is only as reliable as was the person who made it (and you do not even know who it was). If you do uncover an error in the recorded materials, do not add to the problem by writing in your own version or correction. Simply make your own notes, describe the error in your *citations*—references—in order that those who later search will not have the same difficulty, and point out the error to the folks in that office. They may or may not be interested in such help, so do not be disappointed if they seem unconcerned.

At the risk of being repetitious, let us say again: You must not be intimidated by the mass of records in the courthouses. The folks there—and their many predecessors— have been at the business of preserving and cataloging records for a thousand years and more. Their methods are as sound and easy to use as man's inventiveness over the centuries could devise. Only now, with computer technology at hand, are changes of substance and method being made in indexing. So go in, ask for help if you need it, and enjoy the wealth of materials waiting there for you. Too many of us have not.

Throughout every aspect of your search, when you find interesting and important materials, whether during your interviews, at the courthouses, in the libraries, or wherever, always make copies in order that others of your family or friends may enjoy the same records as much as you did. Further, and very important, frequently many years later a re-examination of an old copy will awaken you to an entirely different interpretation from that originally made. In that regard, always be willing to give up old ideas and conclusions, no matter how long you may have held them. We all have had to abandon old notions from time to time.

Writing About Your Family

One day you likely will want to write of your family in a style that will be interesting to others; most of us do. So it is that while the writing of family history is beyond the scope of this handbook, it is necessary that a few words be said about that matter.

Writing takes practice; a lot of it. Such magnificence in historical writings as displayed by the likes of Churchill, Bruce, Fiske, Foote, etc., came only after many years of effort and practice. They were not born with that talent, nor were you, and to be prepared to one day undertake such an effort, however small, you must begin now.

How? Every time you learn a new fact or gain another reference force yourself to write it in sentence form; not later, do it right then. And the lined paper kept in the binder with your family group or unit charts is a good place to enter such sentences. As an example, having known of her death, when you learned of our imaginary Grace McCart's birth, you should have entered those facts not as "Grace McCart, b. 1871, d. Mar. 1, 1950," rather you should have taken the time to write "Grandmother Grace McCart was born in Illinois, probably in 1871, and died there at the age of seventy-nine on March 1, 1950." Then, following that sentence, in an abbreviated form, you should have written the source of that information—e.g., "1880 Census, Illinois, Smith County, Roll 184, page 68, residence 312, family 382." By requiring such simple sentences of yourself, soon you will be writing multiple sentences and then paragraphs. Finally, an assembling of those paragraphs one day will provide a basis for chapters concerning those branches of your family.

In addition, at once you should commence the effort to gather together all mementos, letters, documents, photos, and copies of materials which have to do with your family, wherever they may be. How? Most family collections result from nothing more than requests of relatives for mementos which they no longer want or need. You will be surprised at the materials that relatives will give you simply because you are interested, and nobody in their direct line is.

One researcher, while interviewing an elderly great-uncle, asked if he might have any family items of which the uncle had duplicates or did not need. In response, the old man went to another room, returned with a small box, and told the researcher that his efforts were very much appreciated and since none of the uncle's children had shown any similar interest, while he had no duplicates, the interviewer could have and keep the Civil War discharge certificate of his father, the old veteran's medallions and soldier's hymnal, and the original War of 1812 widow's pension papers of that old soldier's mother! Needless to say, that researcher never again hesitated to ask for items no longer needed. So, after telling them that you have undertaken to gather together the mementos of the family for the benefit of all and that great care will be taken of all mementos, photos, etc., ask all relatives for any family items which they no longer need or want.

> At her Grand daughter's, in Washington Co. Md. on Sunday night last, in the 97th year of her age, ELIZA-BETH ANN ORNDORFF, widow of Major Christian Orndorff, formerly of that county. Thus, full of years, and with an unshaken confidence in the merits of her Redeemer, has this venerable lady paid the last debt to nature. It is supposed that not less than five hundred of her children's children, are now living. Two of her children, one 60, the other 70 years of age, witnessed the solemn ceremony of her interment. Several of her grand children, from 40 to 60 years of age, and great grand children from 20 to 40 years of age, and so on to the sixth generation, followed her to the tomb.

From an 1827 edition of the "National Intelligencer;" an obituary of Elizabeth Ann Orndorff, 92-year-old widow of Revolutionary War Major Christian Orndorff. In 1862, forty-five years after her death, the Orndorff farm would host Antietam's "Bloody Lane." Incredibly and beyond mere coincidence, the fragile newspaper traveled across 170 years and into the possession of co-author and descendant, Mrs. Margaret Grove Driskill!

Perhaps an example of how the gathering of simple data and a few illustrations may be turned into a most interesting story is appropriate. You could and should write just such a story with the facts you will uncover.

As fact and stories unfolded for one researcher, she discovered that the bloodiest day in American history—September 17, 1862, the Battle of Antietam just east of Sharpsburg, Maryland—had included the home of an ancestor. When the battle was over more than 23,000 men from the north and the south had fallen. She learned further that the Grove home, Mt. Airy, was used as a headquarters by Brig. General Alexander S. Webb throughout that month and October, as well, and was thrilled to also learn that the Philip Grove home in Sharpsburg was the site of Robert E. Lee's council of war on the night of September 17, 1862. These great moments in history included HER family!

She began gathering more information and copies of documents, just as you have learned to do from this book, as she had here learned to do, and soon she had before her a story she could write for her family. She gained a USGS "topo" that showed the locations of those properties; she found the cemetery where those very people were buried and took pictures; and she visited the local courthouse and wrote to the Maryland Archives for land records.

Just as we suggested that you do, she searched the Internet and found a book, *Mt. Airy—The Grove Homestead*, by John W. Schildt. Again she was thrilled to learn that on Friday afternoon, October 3, 1862, a horse-drawn carriage approached Mt. Airy. It carried General George B. McClellan and none other than President Abraham Lincoln; they were coming to visit the Fifth Corps, Army of the Potomac, and the wounded men being cared for on the Grove farm. It was at this time that the famous photo of Lincoln at Antietam was taken by Alexander Gardner. What wonderful discoveries! The Grove homestead—her ancestor's house—may been seen in that wonderful photo.

Next, she used the information found in Chapter 3 here and e-mailed the USAMHI (United States Army Military History Institute) in Carlisle, Pennsylvania. Their response was prompt and rewarding; she received a very detailed photographic copy of that great Gardner negative of Lincoln, McClellan, and HER family's house. Though the characters and the places will not be the same, you may make similar discoveries at USAMHI; they have thousands of negatives and pictures of historical significance that they will share with you.

So, dear reader, we urge you not to wait. While the researcher above found an ancestor in the middle of a most historic moment and a great battle, it would have been just as interesting to have found a horse thief or an ordinary farmer in their place in history. In short, your ancestors struggled desperately to settle this great land for you and your family, and it is vitally important that you share their stories with those who come after you.

The wonderful sketch found by our researcher from the 1888 "Battles and Leaders of the Civil War." Here is the "Grove House" in which Lee held a council of war on September 16, 1862. Present with Lee were Confederate Generals D. H. Hill and the immortal "Stonewall Jackson."

Civil War photo of President Lincoln.
In the background is the Grove House, ancestral home of the co-author, Ms. Driskill.

Conclusion

The gathering and study of family history is not only worthwhile, it provides an inner reward and an intellectual challenge seldom found in any other hobby. Not only will you become a detective and an amateur historian, you will learn and appreciate much of human nature and even more about how your own people lived (and died). You will be excited and delighted every time you discover a new branch of your family tree, and will know that but for your efforts, this piece of your history might have remained hidden forever.

As a result of our research efforts, most of us have developed a deep regard and abiding interest in some certain family member or line, which interest has driven us to seek out every last word and scrap of evidence concerning those lives. All of us have come to have a deep respect for the enormous effort that was demanded of and accomplished by our pioneer ancestors. So will you.

They were a strong people—those who struggled through the wars, sometimes through destitution and often through hard times, through the filth of the cities, the snakes and mosquitoes of the Carolina swamps, the heat of west Texas, and the terrible cold of northern Vermont, the long, long, long years—and a good thing it was too; they had an America to build and frontiers to conquer at every turn. Frontiers in science, in the arts, in exploration, in every field of endeavor. Perhaps Churchill said it better than anybody:

> *"We have not traveled all this way across the centuries—across the oceans, across the mountains, across the prairies—because we are made of sugar candy."*

Good luck and best wishes, and may we meet someplace, sometime.

Margaret and Paul
December, 1999

Appendix 1

Forms

This section contains a number of the genealogical forms discussed in this book. The first form is a Pedigree Chart, the second is a Family Unit Chart, and after that follow eleven census forms, from 1790 to 1920, which will assist you in your research. Please note that there are no forms for censuses after 1920, since the 1930 census will not be open to the public until the year 2002—72 years after the taking.

To use any of the forms, simply make as many copies as you need. For inclusion in this book the original forms had to be reduced, so when you make your copies, you might want to enlarge them again (approximately 110-115% of present size) to improve readability and ease of use.

PEDIGREE CHART

Compiler _____

Address _____

_____

Date _____

The first person on this chart is the same person as No. _____ on chart No. _____.

CHART NO. ◯

KEY
ca	about
cont	continuation
b	date of birth
p b	place of birth
m	date of marriage
p m	place of marriage
d	date of death
p.d	place of death

Record dates as day, month, year:
4 July 1776
Record places as city (county) state
Chicago (Cook) Illinois

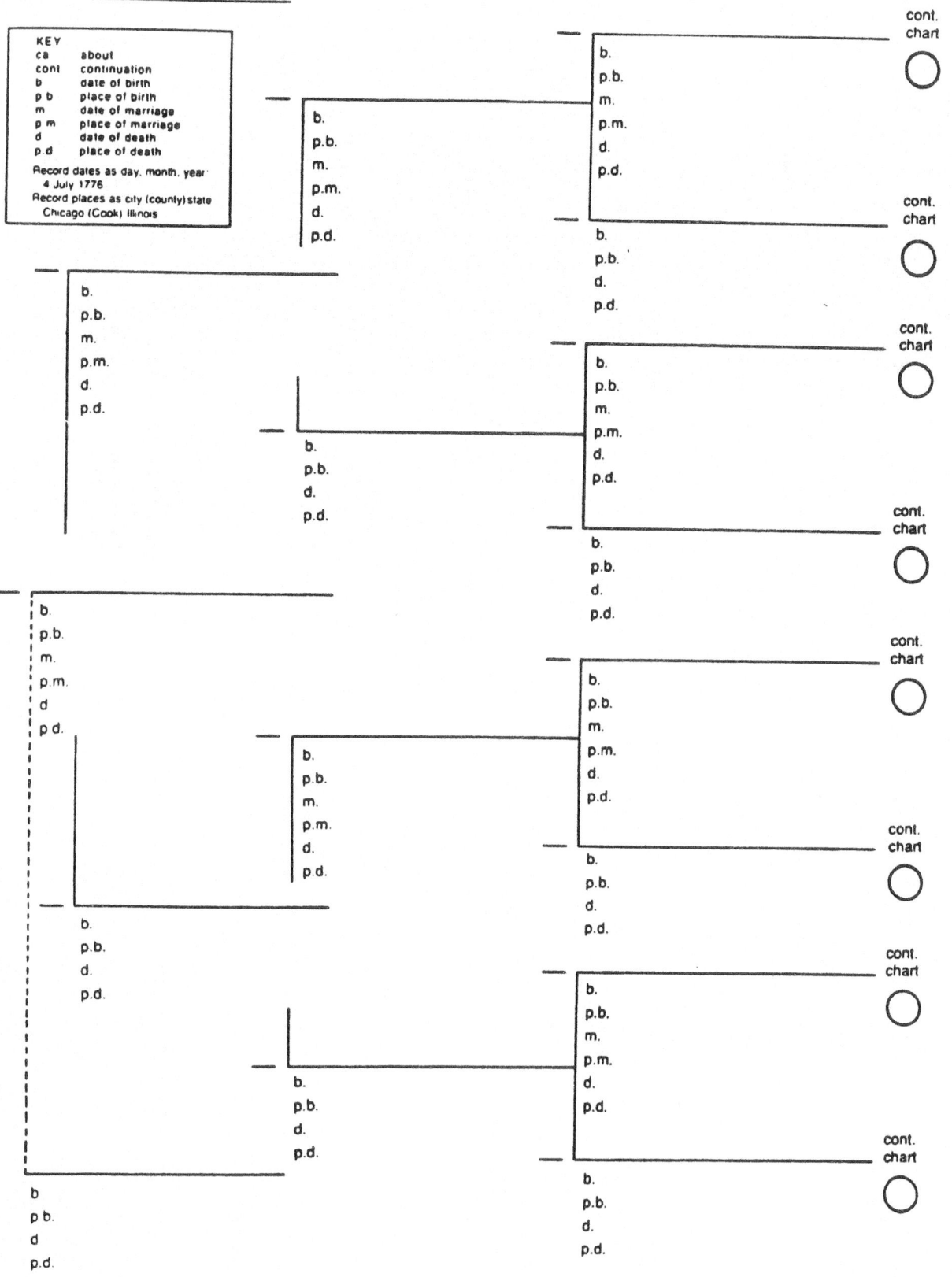

b.
p.b.
m.
p.m.
d.
p.d.

b.
p.b.
m.
p.m.
d.
p.d.

b.
p.b.
m.
p.m.
d.
p.d.

b.
p.b.
m.
p.m.
d
p d

b.
p.b.
m.
p.m.
d.
p.d.

b.
p.b.
d.
p.d.

b.
p.b.
m.
p.m.
d.
p.d.

b.
p.b.
d.
p.d.

b
p b.
d
p.d.

b.
p.b.
m.
p.m.
d.
p.d.

b.
p.b.
d.
p.d.

b.
p.b.
m.
p.m.
d.
p.d.

b.
p.b.
d.
p.d.

cont. chart ◯

cont. chart ◯

cont. chart ◯

cont. chart ◯

cont. chart ◯

cont. chart ◯

cont. chart ◯

cont. chart ◯

b.
p.b.
m.
p.m.
d.
p.d.

b.
p.b.
d.
p.d.

b.
p.b.
m.
p.m.
d.
p.d.

b.
p.b.
d.
p.d.

b.
p.b.
m.
p.m.
d.
p.d.

b.
p.b.
d.
p.d.

b.
p.b.
m.
p.m.
d.
p.d.

b.
p.b.
d.
p.d.

National Genealogical Society, 1921 Sunderland Pl., N.W., Washington, D.C. 20036

PEDIGREE CHART

NAME _____

STREET ADDRESS OR P.O. _____

CITY, STATE, ZIP CODE _____

NO. 1 ON THIS CHART
IS THE SAME AS NO. _____

ON CHART NO. _____

1
BORN
WHERE
WHEN MARRIED
DIED
WHERE
NAME OF HUSBAND OR WIFE

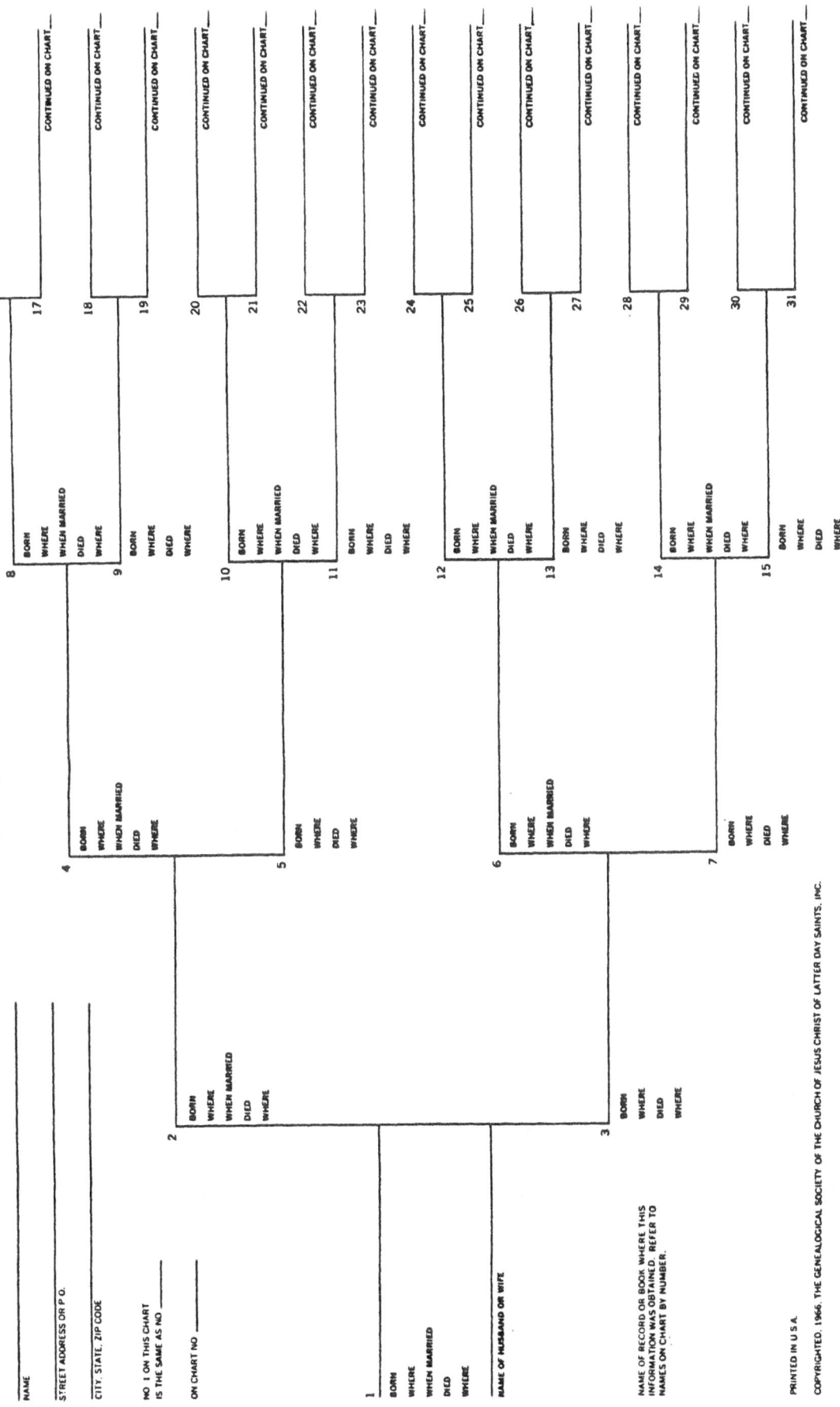

NAME OF RECORD OR BOOK WHERE THIS
INFORMATION WAS OBTAINED. REFER TO
NAMES ON CHART BY NUMBER.

PRINTED IN U.S.A.

COPYRIGHTED, 1966, THE GENEALOGICAL SOCIETY OF THE CHURCH OF JESUS CHRIST OF LATTER DAY SAINTS, INC.

2
BORN
WHERE
WHEN MARRIED
DIED
WHERE

3
BORN
WHERE
DIED
WHERE

4
BORN
WHERE
WHEN MARRIED
DIED
WHERE

5
BORN
WHERE
DIED
WHERE

6
BORN
WHERE
WHEN MARRIED
DIED
WHERE

7
BORN
WHERE
DIED
WHERE

8
BORN
WHERE
WHEN MARRIED
DIED
WHERE

9
BORN
WHERE
DIED
WHERE

10
BORN
WHERE
WHEN MARRIED
DIED
WHERE

11
BORN
WHERE
DIED
WHERE

12
BORN
WHERE
WHEN MARRIED
DIED
WHERE

13
BORN
WHERE
DIED
WHERE

14
BORN
WHERE
WHEN MARRIED
DIED
WHERE

15
BORN
WHERE
DIED
WHERE

16 _____ CONTINUED ON CHART _____

17 _____ CONTINUED ON CHART _____

18 _____ CONTINUED ON CHART _____

19 _____ CONTINUED ON CHART _____

20 _____ CONTINUED ON CHART _____

21 _____ CONTINUED ON CHART _____

22 _____ CONTINUED ON CHART _____

23 _____ CONTINUED ON CHART _____

24 _____ CONTINUED ON CHART _____

25 _____ CONTINUED ON CHART _____

26 _____ CONTINUED ON CHART _____

27 _____ CONTINUED ON CHART _____

28 _____ CONTINUED ON CHART _____

29 _____ CONTINUED ON CHART _____

30 _____ CONTINUED ON CHART _____

31 _____ CONTINUED ON CHART _____

FAMILY UNIT CHART

x = Direct
√ = Ancestc
√ = LDS Temple
Ord. Compl.

PREPARED BY _____   DATE _____

ANCESTRAL CHART #   FAMILY UNIT #

HUSBAND

DATE -- DAY, MONTH, YEAR | OCCUPATION | CITY | COUNTY | STATE or COUNTRY

Born
Christened
Married
Died
Buried
FATHER
MOTHER   OTHER WIVES:

WIFE maiden name

Born
Christened
Died
Buried
FATHER
MOTHER   OTHER HUSBANDS:

X	SEX	CHILDREN	BIRTH			BIRTHPLACE			DATE OF FIRST MARRIAGE	DATE OF DEATH		
√	M/F	Living, Adopted, Dead—In Order of Birth	Day	Month	Year	City	County	St./Cry.	Name of Spouse	City	County	State/Country
1												
2												
3												
4												
5												
6												
7												
8												
9												
10												
11												
12												
13												
14												

1790 CENSUS – UNITED STATES

State _____

Call No. _____

County	City	Page	Head of Family	Free White Males		Free White Females	All Other Persons	Slaves
				16 & up incl. head of families	Under 16	Incl. head of family		

1800–1810 CENSUS — UNITED STATES

State _____ County _____ City _____ Call No. _____

Page	Head of Family	Free White Males					Free White Females					All Others	Slaves	Remarks
		Under 10	10–16	16–26	26–45	45 & Over	Under 10	10–16	16–26	26–45	45 & Over			

1820 CENSUS — UNITED STATES

State _____ County _____ City _____ Call No _____

Page	Head of Family	Free White Males						Free White Females					Foreigners not naturalized	Agriculture	Commerce	Manufactures	Free Colored	Slaves	Remarks
		Under 10	10–16	16–18	16–26	26–45	45 and over	Under 10	10–16	16–26	26–45	45 and over							

1830 - 1840 CENSUS – UNITED STATES

State _____ County _____ City _____ Call No. _____

Page	Head of Family	Free White Males														Free White Females														Slaves	Free Colored	Foreigners not naturalized.
		Under 5	5-10	10-15	15-20	20-30	30-40	40-50	50-60	60-70	70-80	80-90	90-100	Over 100	Under 5	5-10	10-15	15-20	20-30	30-40	40-50	50-60	60-70	70-80	80-90	90-100	Over 100			

1850 CENSUS UNITED STATES

State _____
County _____
Town _____
Township _____
Call No. _____

Page	Dwelling Number	Family Number	Names	Age	Sex	Color	Occupation, etc.	Value - Real Estate	Birthplace	Married within year	School within year	Cannot read or write	Enumeration Date	Remarks

1860 CENSUS UNITED STATES

State _____ County _____ T⌐⌐n/Township _____ P.O. _____ Cell No. _____

Page	Dwelling No.	Family No.	Names	Age	Sex	Color	Occupation, etc.	Value - Real Estate	Value - Personal Property	Birthplace	Married in Year	School in Year	Can't Read or Write	Enumeration Date	Remarks

1870 CENSUS – UNITED STATES

State _____ County _____ Town _____ Township _____ P.O. _____ Call No. _____

Page	Dwelling No.	Family No.	Names	Age	Sex	Color	Occupation, etc.	Value - Real Estate	Value - Personal property	Birthplace	Father Foreign born	Mother Foreign born	Month born in year	Month married in year	School in Year	Can't Read or Write	Eligible to vote	Date of Enumeration

1880 CENSUS – UNITED STATES

State _____ County _____ Township _____ Town _____ Call No. _____

Page	Dwelling No.	Family No.	Names	Color	Sex	Age prior to June 1st	Month of birth if born in census yr.	Relationship to head of house	Single	Married	Widowed	Divorced	Married in census year	Occupation	Miscellaneous Information	Cannot read or write	Place of birth	Place of birth of father	Place of birth of mother	Enumeration Date

1900 CENSUS

Microfilm _____
Roll No. _____

State _____
County _____

Town/Township _____

Supv. Dist. No. _____
Enum. Dist. No. _____

Date _____

Sheet No. _____
Page No. _____

LOCATION				NAME	Relation to head of family	PERSONAL DESCRIPTION									NATIVITY			CITIZENSHIP			OCCUPATION		EDUCATION						
Street	House No.	Dwelling No.	Family No.	of each person whose place of abode on June 1, 1900, was in this family		Color	Sex	Month of birth	Year of birth	Age	Single, married, widowed, divorced	No. of years married	Mother of how many children	Number of these children living	Place of birth	Place of birth of father	Place of birth of mother	Year of immigration to U.S.	No. of years in U.S.	Naturalization	Occupation	No. of months not employed	Attended school (months)	Can read	Can write	Can speak English	Home owned or rented	Home owned free or mortgaged	Farm or house

1910 Census – United States

State _____ County _____ Township or other Division of County _____

Enumeration Date _____ Roll _____ Sheet _____ Dist. _____

(Top portion)

LOCATION			NAME	RELATION	PERSONAL DESCRIPTION								BIRTHPLACE		
House number city or town	Number of dwelling house	Number of family	of each person living in this family on April 15, 1910 (Include every person living on April 15, 1910. Omit children born since April 15, 1910	Relationship of the person to the Head of the family	Sex	Color or race	Age at last birthday.	Single, married, widowed, or divorced	Number of yrs. present marr.	Mother of how many children — Number born	Mother of how many children — Number Now living		Place of birth of this person.	Place of birth of father of this person.	Place of birth of mother of this person.
Line															
1															
2															
3															
4															
5															
6															
7															
8															

(Bottom portion)

CITIZENSHIP		OCCUPATION					EDUCATION			OWNERSHIP OF HOME						REMARKS
Year of immigration to U S	Naturalized or Alien	Trade or profession or particular kind of work done by person, as spinner, salesman, laborer, etc.	General nature of industry, business, or establishment in which person works, as cotton mill, dry goods store, farm, etc.	Whether an employer, employee or working on own account.	If employee — Out of work on April 15, 1910.	If employee — Weeks out of work during year 1909	Able to read?	Able to write?	Attended school any time since Sept 1, 1909	Owned or rented	Owned free or mortgaged	Farm or house	Number of farm schedule	Whether survivor Union, Confederate Army or Navy	Whether blind (both eyes) Whether deaf and dumb	
Line		Speak English; or, if not, language spoken.														
1																
2																
3																
4																
5																
6																
7																
8																

SHEET #_____ A

DEPARTMENT OF COMMERCE-BUREAU OF THE CENSUS

FOURTEENTH CENSUS OF THE UNITED STATES: 1920-POPULATION

STATE_____ SUPERVISOR'S DISTRICT_____

COUNTY_____ ENUMERATION DISTRICT_____

TOWNSHIP OR OTHER DIVISION OF COUNTY_____

NAME OF INCORPORATED PLACE_____ WARD OF CITY_____

FILM SERIES T 625: ROLL_____ NAME OF INSTITUTION_____

ENUMERATOR_____ ENUMERATED ON THE_____DAY OF_____1920

PLACE OF ABODE				NAME	REL.	TENURE		PERSONAL DESCRIPTION				CITIZENSHIP			EDUCATION		
Street, avenue, road, etc.	House number or farm	Number of dwelling house in order of visitation.	Number of family in order of visitation.	of each person whose place of abode on January 1, 1920, was in this family. Enter surname first, then given and middle initial if any. Omit children born since January 1, 1920.	To head of household.	Home owned or rented	If owned, free or mortgaged.	Sex.	Color or race.	Age at last birthday.	Single, married, widowed, or divorced	Year of Immigration to the United States.	Naturalized or alien.	If naturalized, year of naturalization.	Attended school any time since 1 Sept 1919	Whether able to read.	Whether able to write.
1	2	3	4	5	6	7	8	9	10	11	12	13	14	15	16	17	18
				1													
				2													
				3													
				4													
				5													
				6													
				7													
				8													
				9													
				10													
				11													
				12													
				13													
				14													
				15													

FILM READ AT_____

BY_____ DATE_____

NOTES

NATIVITY AND MOTHER TONGUE Place of birth of each person and parents of each person enumerated. If born in the United States, give the state or territory. If foreign born, give the place of birth and, in addition, the mother tongue.						Whether able to speak English.	OCCUPATION		Employer, salary or wage worker, or working as own account.	Number of farm schedule.
PERSON		FATHER		MOTHER			Trade, profession, or particular kind of work done, as *spinner, salesman, laborer,* etc.	Industry, business, or establishment in which at work, as *cotton mill, dry goods store, farm,* etc.		
Place of Birth	Mother Tongue	Place of Birth	Mother Tongue	Place of Birth	Mother Tongue					
19	20	21	22	23	24	25	26	27	28	29
1										
2										
3										
4										
5										
6										
7										
8										
9										
10										
11										
12										
13										
14										
15										

Appendix 2

The National Archives

As mentioned in Chapter 2, page 15 and onwards, the researcher can procure by mail copies of such valuable records as veteran or widow pension applications, land-bounty warrants and more from the National Archives. To request a search of the Archives you will need to use form NATF-80. To receive form NATF-80 free of charge, go to the web site, **www.nara.gov** or write to the following address:

> *General Reference Branch (NNRG-P)*
> *National Archives and Records Administration*
> *7th and Pennsylvania Avenue NW.*
> *Washington, DC 20408*

You will need to fill out a separate NATF-80 form for each individual whose records you want searched, so order several. Your forms will arrive complete with all information you will need on how to fill them out, how to pay etc. The types of records that can be searched are:

Pension Application Files

These are the most useful records for genealogical research and contain most complete information on a man's military career. The National Archives recommend that you first request the Pension Application Files.

The Pension Application Files are based on Federal (*not State*) service before World War I. Pensions based on Confederate service were authorized by some southern states but until 1959 not by the Federal Government.

Bounty-land Warrant Files

Request when no pension file exists. If the veteran's service was during the Revolutionary war, bounty-land warrant files have been consolidated with pension application files and can be obtained by requesting the pension files only.

Bounty-land warrant files are based again on Federal, and not State, service before 1856. The information in the files is similar to that in pension application files. Additionally these files usually give the veteran's age and place of residence at the time of application.

Military Service Records

These only rarely contain family information. The Military Service Records are based on service in one of the following United States military organizations:

- Army: officers who served before June 30, 1917
  enlisted men who served before October 31, 1912.
- Navy: officers who served before 1903
  enlisted men who served before 1886.

- Marine Corps: officers who served before 1896
  enlisted men who served before 1905.
- Confederate Armed Forces:
  officers and enlisted men who served between 1861 and 1865.
- Volunteers who fought in various wars from the Revolutionary war through the Philippine Insurrection, covering the period from 1775 to 1902.

For records relating to service in World War I, II, or later, write to:
National Personnel Records Center (Military Records)
NARA
9700 Page Boulevard
St. Louis, MO 63132

Census Records

The National Archives does not search census records, but it can provide copies of specific pages of Federal population census schedules. Use form NATF-81 to request the copies.

Minimum information you will need to provide:
- name of the individual listed
- page number
- census year
- county and state

For the 1880 through 1910 censuses you will need to provide the enumeration district as well.

Ship Passenger Arrival Records

The National Archives has inbound Federal Ship Passenger Arrival Records. A number of these have been indexed, others have not. Use form NATF-82 to request a search of these records.

The following major indexes of passenger lists exist:

Baltimore	1820-1952
Boston	1848-1891 and 1902-1920
New Orleans	1853-1952
New York	1820-1846 and 1897-1948
Philadelphia	1800-1948
Minor ports	1820-1874 and 1890-1924

Notice that no law required that arrival records be kept for persons entering the US by land via Canada or Mexico, or for outbound ship passengers.

To have the indexes searched you will need to provide the following information:
- full name of the passenger
- port of entry
- approximate date of arrival

To have unindexed passenger lists searched you will need to supply the following minimum information:
- full name of the passenger
- name of the ship

- port of entry
- approximate date of arrival
or
- full name of the passenger
- port of embarkation
- port of entry
- exact date of arrival

For unindexed lists after 1892, you will need to provide:
- full name of passenger
- names and ages of accompanying passengers, if any
- name of the ship
- port of entry
- exact date of arrival

In addition, you can also order copies of an entire passenger list or search the records yourself (or have them searched by a representative) if they are too voluminous for the National Archives staff to search.

Naturalization Records

These are separate from passenger arrival lists. The National Archives has copies of naturalization papers for the years 1798 to 1906 for:

Massachusetts,
New Hampshire,
Rhode Island,
Maine,

in addition to original records for the District of Columbia for the years 1802 to 1926.

For information on citizenship granted elsewhere though September 26, 1906 write to the Federal, State or municipal court that issued the naturalization. For information on naturalizations after September 26, 1906, write to:

The Immigration and Naturalization Service
Washington, DC 20536

National Archives Regional Archives System

You may visit the following regional archives to research Federal population census records dating from 1790 to 1910. However, the regional offices do not offer the mail order photocopying service of the General Reference Branch (address at the beginning of this section) . Call for current hours of operation. Additional information is available from the web site: **www.nara.gov/nara/gotonara/html**

National Archives - **Alaska Region**
   654 West 3rd Avenue
   Anchorage, AK 99501
   Phone: (907) 271-2441
   Areas served: *Alaska.*

National Archives-**Central Plains Region**
   2313 East Bannister Road
   Kansas City, MO 64131
   Phone: (816) 926-6272
   Areas served: *Iowa, Kansas, Missouri, Nebraska.*

National Archives - **Great Lakes Region**
  7358 South Pulaski Road
  Chicago, IL 60629
  Phone: (312) 581-7816
  Areas served: *Illinois, Indiana, Michigan, Minnesota, Ohio, Wisconsin.*

National Archives - **Mid Atlantic Region**
  9th & Market Streets, Room 1350
  Philadelphia, PA 19107
  Phone: (215) 597-3000
  Areas served: *Delaware, Maryland, Pennsylvania, Virginia, West Virginia.*

National Archives - **New England Region**
  380 Trapelo Road
  Waltham, MA 02154
  Phone: (617) 647-8100
  Areas served: *Connecticut, Maine, Massachusetts, New Hampshire, Rhode Island, Vermont.*

National Archives - **Northeast Region**
  Building 22, Military Ocean Terminal
  Bayonne, NJ 07002-5388
  Phone: (201) 823-7545
  Areas served: *New Jersey, New York, Puerto Rico, Virgin Islands.*

National Archives - **Pacific Southwest Region**
  24000 Avila Road
  Laguna Niguel, CA 92677-6719
  Phone: (714) 643-4241
  Areas served: *Arizona; southern Californian counties of Imperial, Inyo, Kern, Los Angeles, Orange, Riverside, San Bernardino, San Diego, San Luis Obispo, Santa Barbara, Ventura; and Clark County, Nevada.*

National Archives - **Pacific Northwest Region**
  6125 Sand Point Way
  Seattle, WA 98115
  Phone: (206) 526-6507
  Areas served: *Idaho, Oregon, Washington.*

National Archives - **Pacific Sierra Region**
  1000 Commodore Drive
  San Bruno, CA 94066
  Phone: (415) 876-9009
  Areas served: *Northern California, Hawaii, Nevada (except for Clark County), Pacific Ocean Area.*

National Archives - **Rocky Mountain Region**
  Building 48, Denver Regional Center
  Denver, CO 80225
  Phone: (303) 236-0817
  Areas served: *Colorado, Montana, North Dakota, South Dakota, Utah, Wyoming.*

National Archives - **Southeast Region**
  1557 St. *Joseph Avenue*
  East Point, GA 30344
  Phone: (404) 763-7477
  Areas served: *Alabama, Georgia, Florida, Kentucky, Mississippi, North Carolina, South Carolina, Tennessee.*

National Archives - **Southwest Region**
  501 West Felix Street
  Fort Worth, TX 76115
  Phone: (817) 334-5525
  Areas served: *Arkansas, Louisiana, New Mexico, Oklahoma, Texas.*

Appendix 3

Societies, Periodicals and Directories

Societies

Board for Certification of Genealogists
    P.O. Box 14291
    Washington, DC 20044
    http://www.genealogy.org/~bcg

Family History Library (LDS)
    35 NW Temple
    Salt Lake City, UT 84150
    Tel: (801) 240-2331
    http://www.familysearch.org

Federation of Genealogical Societies
    P.O. Box 200940
    Austin, TX 78720-0940
    Tel: (512) 336-2731
    http://www.fgs.org

International Association of Jewish
Genealogical Societies
    104 Franklin Avenue
    Yonkers, NY 10705-2808
    http://www.jewishgen.org

National African-American Historical &
Genealogical Society
    P.O. Box 73086
    Washington, DC 20056-3086
    Tel: (202) 234-5330
    http://www.everton.com/oe2-
7/afamlist.htm

National Society, Daughters of the
American Revolution
    1776 D Street, NW
    Washington, DC 20006-5392
    Tel: (202) 879-3229
    http://dar.library.net

National Society, Sons of the American
Revolution
    1000 South Fourth Street
    Louisville, KY 40203
    Tel: (502) 589-1776
    http://www.sar.org

Palatines to America
    Box 101, Capital University
    Columbus, OH 43209
    http://www.genealogy.org/~palam

Sons of Confederate Veterans
    P.O. Box 59
    Columbia, TN 38402-0059
    Tel: 1-800 MY DIXIE
    http://www.scv.org

United Daughters of the Confederacy
    328 North Boulevard
    Richmond, VA 23220-4057
    Tel: (804) 355-1636
    http://www.hqudc.org

Periodicals

Genealogical Helper
P.O. Box 368
Logan, UT 84323-0368
Tel: (800) 443-6325
http://www.everton.com

Heritage Quest
593 West 100 North
Bountiful, UT 84010
(800) 760-2455
http://www.heritagequest.com

Directories

American Association for State and Local History
1717 Church Street
Nashville, TN 37203-2991
Tel: (615) 320-3203
http://www.aaslh.org

Association of Professional Genealogists
P.O. Box 40393
Denver, CO 80204-0393
http://www.apgen.org/directory.html

Directory of Family Associations
Genealogical Publishing Co., Inc.
1001 N. Calvert Street
Baltimore, MD 21202
Tel: (800) 296-6687

Miscellaneous Agencies

BLM
Bureau of Land Management
Eastern States
7450 Boston Blvd.
Springfield, VA 22153-3121
(703) 440-1600
http://www.blm.gov

Library of Congress
101 Independence Avenue, SE
Washington, DC 20540
(202) 707-5000
http://lcweb.loc.gov/homepage/lchp.html

USAMHI
United States Army Military History Institute
Special Collections
22 Ashburn Drive
Carlisle, PA 17013-5008
(717) 245-3434
http://carlisle-www.army.mil/usamhi/PhotoDB.html

USGS
United States Geological Survey
508 National Center
Reston, VA 20192
(888) 275-8747
http://mapping.usgs.gov/

Glossary

Abstract

A summary of the most important information in a document, article or book. For instance, an abstract of a deed may relate the names of the people involved, the consideration, a summarized description of the property, warranties, and the nature of the rights transferred, yet not include the legal jargon, the acknowledgment, and the names of the witnesses. (See Extract and Summary)

Administrator (male), Administratrix (female)

A person designated by a court to represent someone who died without an operative will. Usually bonded, an administrator sees to it that the burial is paid for, receivables collected, that debts, taxes, and court costs are paid, and, finally, that the remaining assets of the deceased are properly distributed among his or her heirs. (See Intestate and Bond)

Adoption

A legal process whereby, usually to the exclusion of the natural parents, people make someone else's child legally their own. The adoptive parents undertake the duties of natural parents to that child, and the adopted child gains the rights, privileges and duties of a natural child.

Affidavit

A written or printed declaration of facts, made voluntarily and under oath before a person legally empowered to administer oaths, such as a judge, justice of the peace, a notary public, or a lawyer.

Affinity

The relationship between people whose kinship is by marriage and not "by blood." The relationship between a husband and his wife's relatives is said to be by affinity. (See Consanguinity)

Aforesaid, beforesaid, abovesaid, said

Often used in legal documents, these words refer to a person, object, proposition, or premise previously mentioned in the same document.

Ancestor

Any person from whom one is directly and linearly descended. (See Collateral)

Ancillary

A proceeding which supplements or complements another proceeding. When, for instance, a decedent owned land not only in the county where he or she lived, but in another county as well, the administration in the second county is said to be ancillary to that performed in the county of residence. (See Decedent)

Appraisal, Appraisement
An assessment of the value of property, real or personal. In genealogy, the term usually refers to the evaluation of the assets of a dead person.

Archives
Usually, the place of keeping for records, writings, mementos, and artifacts having to do with the history of a nation, state, community, group of people, or a family. The term is also used to refer to the actual records, writings, and mementos.

Asset
Any property, including real property (real estate, interests in land) and personalty (personal property). Personalty is all property other than real estate. In addition to tangible personal property—cattle, refrigerators, tools, etc.—intangible property such as stocks, bonds, negotiable writings, legal claims against others, and accounts receivable are also considered personalty.

Banns, Banns of Matrimony
A requirement in the Church of England and often in the Catholic Church, that a marriage be announced publicly. The announcement is made at a regular service in the church on three consecutive Sundays prior to the proposed date of ceremony. The purpose is to allow time for anyone to come forth who believes there is a valid reason why the marriage should not take place.

Beneficiary
Someone who gains profit, advantage, or benefits from another (the benefactor). Someone who inherits from somebody else is said to be that person's beneficiary.

Bond
A sum of money, pledge of credit, insurance guarantee or other thing of value deposited, usually with a court, as assurance that a proposed act is proper or that one will faithfully and properly perform certain duties. Administrators of estates are bonded—provide financial assurance—that they will properly attend to and complete the business of the dead person.

Cenotaph
A monument to one who is deceased, erected elsewhere than at the place of burial. (see Epitaph)

Census
An official counting (enumeration) of all people within a political subdivision (city, county, state, nation). Formerly, a census was taken solely by census-takers (enumerators) who went from door to door listing the names, ages, occupations, etc. of the occupants of each dwelling.

Chattel
Any item of property that is not real estate. Chattels are divided into chattels real and chattels personal. Chattels real are tangible goods (guns, dishes, furniture), while chattels personal are intangible property such as accounts receivable, stocks, bonds, etc.

City

In the U.S., a municipality, usually larger than a town or village, which governs itself under a charter or by authority granted or given over by a state. Thus, a city is not part of a county yet governs itself in much the same way a county does.

Civil War

That American conflict, also called "The War Between The States" and "The War of the Rebellion," which took place between 1861 and 1865. Other nations (including England, 1642-1646) also have had internal conflicts called civil wars.

Clear and Convincing

A measure of proof beyond "preponderance of evidence." In genealogy, that quantum of evidence that convinces someone else that one hypothesis is almost certainly correct and that no other solution is likely to be found. (see Preponderance of Evidence)

Collateral Branches, Collateral Lines

All relatives who are related to you by blood but not directly (linearly): aunts, uncles, nieces, nephews, etc. The children, grandchildren, etc. of a brother or sister of one of your ancestors, also are your collateral lines. (See Affinity and Consanguinity)

Colonial

Refers to the period before the American Revolution during which the first thirteen states of the United States were still English colonies. Also refers to the style of architecture, dress, etc. prevalent then in British North America.

Consanguinity

Meaning "of the same blood," you are related by consanguinity to all persons who descend from an ancestor of yours. (See Affinity and Collateral Branches)

Consideration

Refers to anything of value (money, assets, services) that is given in payment for property, real or personal. Love and affection are sufficient consideration—payment—for property if the grantor and grantee so agree.

Constable

A public officer of a town or section of a county whose duties include matters of the peace, the service of writs, and the custody of jurors. While the powers of a constable varies from state to state, he or she usually has considerably less authority than a sheriff. Formerly the constable was a more important officer of the law than now, and the title and office were actively sought after.

County

In the U.S., a political subdivision of a state, created to facilitate the administration of justice and law, and to permit limited self-government and determination.

County Seat

The town or city within which the county buildings and courts are found, and where the principal business of the county is carried out.

Decedent, Deceased

A dead person; the term usually describes someone who has recently died.

Deed

Any written instrument, signed and delivered, that conveys an interest in real estate from one person to another.

Descendant

Someone who linearly descends from another, no matter through how many generations. Sometimes the term also refers to all those to whom property descends at a death, no matter what the kinship.

Digitizing

A word new to the end of the 20th century meaning to scan or photograph electronically and to preserve that object scanned by storing it, again, electronically. An elctronic method by which writings may be rendered more readable, e.g., "A digital camera is very helpful for improving the resolution of old documents."

Direct Index

An index (often now computerized) to the records of deeds and mortgages, usually kept in a courthouse. The Direct Index lists, in alphabetical order by surname, the grantors or mortgagors. Often also called the Grantor Index. (see Reverse Index)

Discharge

As a verb, to discharge a duty or obligation means to fulfill that which is required of one. As a noun, a discharge is the document that releases one from military or other service and also provides evidence that he or she has performed certain military duties.

Dower

A part of or interest in the estate of a decedent that is reserved by law for the maintenance and support of the surviving spouse during his or her life. Originally the term dower referred to the interests of a surviving spouse in real estate gained by the deceased during their marriage.

Dowry

The property a woman brings to a marriage. Originally, the dowry became the sole property of the husband at their marriage.

E-mail

Electronic mail. Send and receive messages over the Internet.

Enumeration, Enumerator

Enumeration literally means a counting or numbering, and the person who does the numbering is the enumerator. In genealogy, the term enumeration usually refers to a census, and the enumerators are the people who "take" the census.

Epitaph

A statement, quotation or verse on a monument or headstone, usually in praise of the deceased.

Estate

All assets, real and personal, belonging to a person, whether living or dead. In genealogy, the term usually refers to the assets of a deceased person at the time of his or her death.

Evidence

In genealogy, every word, writing, memento, artifact, and state of being that in any way whatever tends to demonstrate, link or establish lineage is evidence.

Executor (male), Executrix (female)

A person (or persons) who was named in a decedent's will (and who also was found acceptable by a court) to carry out the terms of that will. The duties of an executor or executrix include arranging the burial of the dead person, collecting all assets owing to him or her, paying all debts and taxes, distributing the remaining assets as prescribed by the will, and then closing the estate.

Extract

A section from a document, letter, book or article, usually taken whole and verbatim from the original. This in contrast to an abstract which repeats only part of the information, or a summary which condenses the information. (See Abstract and Summary)

Foster, Fostered out

A foster parent is someone who carries out the duties of raising a child without legally claiming that child as his or her own. Fostering out is an ancient Irish custom which was carried to the Americas and here modified to an arrangement where a child was given into the custody of another and, in exchange for care and keeping, is expected to perform the duties expected of a natural child. (See Adoption)

French and Indian War

Conflict between England and its American colonies against France and its allied Indian Nations. The French and Indian War started with a series of incidents in 1754 and ended with the defeat of the French forces at Quebec in 1760, thus rendering Canada an English colony.

Genealogy

Genealogy is the study of family history and relationships, both by blood and by marriage. A "genealogy" is a statement, diagram, or summary of kinship.

Genesis

In genealogy, genesis refers to the beginnings and political parentage of any governmental subdivision, specifically those counties or states which were divided up into new counties or states.

Grand-

In genealogy, the prefix "grand" refers to the generation prior to your parents. Thus, the mother of your mother is your grandmother, and her sisters and brothers, your great-aunts and great-uncles, are often called "grand-aunt" and "grand-uncle."

Grantor/Grantee Indexes

Indexes to deeds compiled alphabetically in the surnames of the sellers (a Grantor Index) and in the names of the buyers or transferees (a Grantee Index). (see Direct Index and Reverse Index)

Great-

In genealogy, the prefix "great" refers to your ancestors prior to your grandparents and to aunts and uncles prior to the generation of your parents. Each generation more distant from your grandparents has another "great" added. Thus the mother of your grandfather is your great-grandmother, and her father (your grandfather's grandfather) is your great-great-grandfather.

Heir

Presently used to designate any person entitled to inherit from another by right of descent or relationship, whether the death is testate or intestate. Formerly, an heir was someone who inherited by virtue of a statute or law rather than by the provisions of a will.

Hereinafter, Hereinbefore

Legal jargon used to refer to a term or provision within the same document, e.g. "... being the tract hereinafter described as the property of L. Y. Drake" or "... being the persons hereinbefore mentioned."

Holographic Will

A will written, dated, and signed entirely by the decedent in his own hand. Usually, to be legally admissible a holographic will must have been kept in such a place and maintained with a degree of care that its importance to the decedent seems certain.

Inchoate Rights

Any interest in real estate which has not yet been realized or vested in the owner. In genealogy, the term usually refers to a wife's intangible interests in the real estate of her husband during his life, which may ripen into dower rights at his death. (See Dower)

Indentured Servants

In the American colonies an indenture was a written contract by which a free person would promise to serve someone else as his servant for a term of usually five to seven years or until about the age of twenty-five. In exchange for his or her work, the indentured servant usually received transportation across the ocean and certain minimal benefits (clothes, grain, small tracts of land, etc.) at the end of the term.

Indian Wars

The term used to denote the many military conflicts with the American Indians which took place during the last half of the nineteenth century, generally in the western states and territories.

Instant (Inst.)

A term often used in early correspondence, meaning the current month. As an example, a person responding on July 20 to a letter received on July 5 might write: "I acknowledge your letter of the 5th Instant." (See Ultimo)

Internet

Electronic network that connects the hosts together so that one may go from one web page to another.

Intestate

When a person dies without a valid will, he or she is said to have died intestate. The opposite of intestate is testate, which means with a will. (see Administrator, Administratrix)

Inventory

In genealogy, an inventory is usually the list an administrator or executor has caused to be made of all property belonging to a decedent at the time of his or her death. (See Appraisal / Appraisement)

Journals, Journal Entries; see Minutes, Minute Books.

Justice of the Peace

A judicial officer of reduced authority, usually having jurisdiction over minor crimes, misdemeanors, and matters of the peace. A justice of the peace was an officer of great importance before modern transportation facilitated trips about the county by a sheriff or his deputies.

Kin, Kinship

A loosely defined term referring to any and all of one's relations, be they by affinity, consanguinity, or by law.

Korean Conflict

The conflict between North Korea (and Communist China) and the United States which took place between 1950 and 1953.

Land Grant

In genealogy, a land grant refers to the document or the act whereby a government conveys an interest in land to an individual, corporation or institution. Generally, but not always, the land concerned had not been previously titled to another person.

Lease

A contract whereby, in exchange for something of value, one person grants another certain rights, duties and privileges in the use of a tract of land (or a building, or other property) for a specific period of time. At the end of that term all rights revert back to the original owner.

Letter Patent; see Patent.

Levy

As a verb, to levy a tax means to impose a tax, as in "The colony levied a tax of 1 shilling on each horse used in farming, the same payable to the circuit court in February of each year." As a noun, a levy is an imposition or collection of a tax.

Liability

A liability is any obligation, debt, or duty to pay or to perform to another person, firm, corporation or government.

Lien

When A fails to pay for services rendered or goods supplied by B, B then often has a right to place a lien (a claim) against some of A's assets, usually against personal property. To be valid under most state's laws, the lien must be written, acknowledged and recorded.

Lineage
Your lineage is your line of descent from your ancestors, revealing the relationship between you, your ancestors and your descendants. The terms "stock" or pedigree usually are synonymous with lineage.

Litigation
The act of settling differences through advocacy and the use of the court system.

Majority; see Of Age.

Manor
Presently, a manor refers to a house that is larger or more grand than average. In early times a manor was a grant of a sizable tract of land by the crown, usually to a nobleman or noblewoman.

Marriage Bond
A pledge to pay money or something of value in the event that it is later learned that one of the partners to a marriage was not legally qualified to have married.

Mexican War
Conflict between the United States and Mexico which took place between 1846 and 1848.

Microfiche, Microfilm
A space-saving way to store copies of original documents, books, etc. In the case of microfilm, the older of the two processes, each page is photographed on a roll of film with usually one page of the original document in each frame. In the case of microfiche, a number of pages are greatly reduced in size and placed on a single sheet of film. (Also see Digitizing)

Militia
An armed body of citizens, organized by a state or (early) a colony and, as opposed to an army, active only in cases of civil obedience, local emergency or danger to the citizenry.

Minutes, Minute Books (Orders, Order Books, Journals, Journal Entries)
The minutes are the official records of the sessions of a judicial court, made by the clerks of that court and collected in the minute books.

Mortgage Deed (Mortgagors, Mortgagees)
A formal, signed, and acknowledged document by which a borrower (mortgagor) transfers the title of his or her property to a lender (mortgagee) as security for a loan of money or other thing of value. When the mortgagor (borrower) has paid the debt as agreed, the mortgagee (lender) then will give the property back, or "release" the title. A mortgage is similar to a deed of trust, except that in a deed of trust the title is transferred to a third party agreeable to both lender and borrower. That third party releases the title back to the mortgagor upon being informed that the debt has been repaid as agreed.

Nativity
In genealogy, nativity means that place where one was born.

Naturalization
The legal procedure by which the government of one country grants citizenship to a person from another country.

Nuncupative Will
An oral will, dictated by one who is dying and realizes it, which words are written down soon after the death and signed by the person who witnessed and heard the words. Early, on the frontier and in sparsely settled areas, when death often came quickly, nuncupative wills were more common than now.

Obituary
An article or notice in a newspaper, periodical, or magazine describing the life, accomplishments, and death of someone who has recently died.

Of Age, Of Majority
The age at which a child becomes an adult, i.e. presumed able and entitled to manage his or her own affairs and enjoy the full civic privileges and rights afforded by his or her government. These days the achievement of eighteen or twenty-one years is necessary for a child to be considered to have come "of age." In the past, fourteen or even twelve years sometimes was considered old enough.

Orders, Order books; see Minutes, Minute Books.

Outcry
Formerly, a sale held by shouting an offer to sell from the courthouse steps to all who might accept the offer and buy. Now, usually a public sale by auction held at a place determined by the owners or by a court.

Patent
In genealogy, a document by which a government, state or federal, grants public land; in early records the term "Letters Patent" frequently appears.

Pedigree
One's lineage or the line of ancestry by which one descends; a chart, account, register, or drawing of one's ancestry.

Per Stirpes
Latin for "by roots" or "by the stock"; to inherit that which an ancestor would have inherited had the ancestor been living. For example, when a granddaughter inherits from her grandmother what her father would have inherited had he outlived his mother, she is said to have "taken per stirpes."

Personalty, Personal Property
All property other than real estate. (see Assets)

Political Subdivision
A term used to describe a division of a larger political boundary or governmental institution, e.g., A county usually is a political subdivision of a state, and a township usually is a political subdivision of a county.

Poll

People singly considered ("poll" originally meant "head"), as in a "poll tax" where a tax is levied on each individual (on each head).

Polls

The place where people cast ballots; a voting place.

Precinct

In America, usually a rather small area in a town or city designated as an election or voting district.

Preponderance of Evidence

A measure of proof. When the evidence tending to prove one hypothesis outweighs, even minimally, the evidence tending to prove a contrary hypothesis, the first hypothesis is said to prevail by a preponderance of evidence. In genealogy, preponderance of evidence is the measure of proof thought sufficient by some, but not all researchers to establish lineage. (see Clear and Convincing)

Primogeniture

The superior and exclusive right of the first born male to succeed to the family property at the death of the head of the family. A doctrine which prevailed widely in the early colonial estates by which the eldest son, or his eldest son, etc., inherited the family property to the exclusion of all sisters, brothers, widows, etc., without regard to need.

Probate, Probate Courts

Probate usually means the legal process by which a will is proved and enforced, but it may refer to any legal process involving estates. Probate courts generally have jurisdiction in matters of death, orphans, adoption, children, lunacy, etc.

Quit-claim

Often imprecisely called a quit-claim deed; an instrument by which one transfers whatever interest he or she may have in some property, usually real estate, to someone else.

Reader

In genealogy, the optical equipment used to read microfilm or microfiche.

Real Estate, Real Property, Realty

Interests in or ownership of land, as opposed to personal property.

Record (to record)

The act of entering any document or writing into the public records by a clerk, recorder, register of deeds, etc., in accordance with a "recording statute." Recording is an innovation peculiar to the American colonies and was not previously known in England.

Redemptioner

Someone who promised his or her labor to a speculator in payment—redemption—usually for transportation to the colonies (and occasionally for some additional compensation). (See Indentured Servant)

Revolutionary War
The conflict between the American Colonies and England which took place between 1775 and 1783 and which resulted in the formation of the United States.

Scribe, Scrivener
A writer. Before literacy was widespread, a scribe was someone whose occupation was writing for others. The surname Scribner derives from the term.

Search Engine
A program that searches documents for "keywords" you want to find. A list of documents containing these keywords are then displayed for your selection.

Section; see Township.

Sheriff
Usually, the chief administrative and peace officer of a county. His duties consist of assisting all courts of general jurisdiction, summoning juries, serving writs and executing court orders. The office of sheriff is an ancient one, known in England before the 12th century. There the "High Sheriff" had wide authority and jurisdiction within a county, and spoke for the crown, the courts, and government in general.

Sibling
From the early Saxon "sibb" which meant a relative or kinsman. Now the term is used only to refer to brothers and sisters.

Spanish-American War
Conflict between the United States and Spain which took place in 1898.

Spouse
One's wife or husband.

Stock
In genealogy, one's ancestry or lineage, from which arises the expression, "That precious little girl surely is from good stock."

Summary
A writing which, with different wording, sets forth the significant portions of another document, article, book, or source. (See Abstract and Extract)

Surety
Someone who gives assurance that another person will pay, appear, or do as agreed or ordered. Usually a surety posts personal credit, a "surety bond", consisting of money or something of value as a guarantee. (see Bond)

Testate
Death with a will, as opposed to intestate, which means death without a will. (See Executor, Executrix)

Tithe, Tithable
Early, a tax-like charge of ten percent to the benefit of the church. In America, the tithe usually was based upon benefits and income derived from land and its use. One is tithable when one is legally obligated to pay tithes.

Title

The word title has two meanings. In the context of real estate and personal property, to "hold title" to something means that one owns that object.   Socially, a title designates a measure of respect or dignity due to a person, e.g., Mr., Mrs., Lord, Judge, etc.

Town

Usually a civil and political subdivision of a county. In New England, a town usually has the powers and authority only accorded to counties in other states. In some states, a town is a village or hamlet within a township.

Township

In lands previously belonging to the U.S. government, a township is a division of land 6 miles long on each side, containing 36 sections of 640 acres (1 square mile) each. In some states, a township refers to a political subdivision of a county and it may or may not consist of 36 square miles.

Transcript

A verbatim record or exact copy of a document, book, or other writing; e.g. "A transcript of the county's Marriage Records was made available to researchers."

Trust deed

See Mortgage Deed.

Ultimo (Ult.)

A term often used in early correspondence; ultimo is short for the Latin "ultimo mense" which means "in the last month." As an example, a person responding in March to a letter received on February 17 might write: "I received your note of the 17th ult." (see Instant)

URL

Uniform Resource Locator. It is the addres of a website. It usually begins with "http://"

Vendee, Vendor

A vendee is a buyer and a vendor is a seller of personal property (personalty).

Veteran

In genealogy, anyone who served in any military or militia unit (under federal, state or territorial government) for any period of time, and who was honorably separated from that service unit. It makes no difference whether the service was voluntary or by conscription (draft).

Vital Statistics

Usually refers to the data maintained by government—state or federal—on births, deaths, and marriages. "Bureaus of Vital Statistics" have been operating in every state since the early years of the twentieth century and are open to the public.

War of 1812

The conflict between the United States and Great Britain which took place between 1812 and 1814.

Ward
A political subdivision of a city or town, having quite limited jurisdiction in matters of voting and elections, sanitary regulations, fire and police protection, and enumerations.

Warranty Deed
A written document transferring interests in land and containing specific warranties concerning the extent of the rights transferred. The most common deeds in this country, warranty deeds contain a complete description of the property, set forth the names of the buyers and the sellers, are acknowledged ("notarized", "sworn to"), almost always recorded, and often, especially early, contain a recital of the consideration given in exchange for the property.

Will
A formal writing, carefully governed by all states, by which a person (a testator or testatrix) directs and sets forth his or her wishes concerning the disposition of their property and estate at death. A will usually names and empowers an executor or executrix; gives directions concerning burial, collection of receivables and payment of bills and taxes; names all beneficiaries and disposes of the remainder of the estate. To be legal, a will quite usually must be signed, acknowledged, and witnessed. (See Executor, Executrix; Nuncupative Wills; and Holographic Wills)

World War I
World-wide conflict of 1914-1918, in which the United States took part from 1917 until 1918.

World War II
World-wide conflict of 1939-1945 in which the United States took part from December of 1941 until August of 1945.

World Wide Web
Multimedia database of information n the internet.

Writ
In genealogy, any order by a court in the name of a government—federal, state or local—addressed to a sheriff or other law officer. Often, a writ will direct an officer to notify someone of an action filed against him or her and instruct such persons to appear at a certain time and place to answer to the charge or complaint filed. Writs are common genealogical source documents.

WWW
Acronym for World Wide Web.

Index

A

ABSTRACTS, 37
ACCOUNTS RECEIVABLE, 64
ADMINISTRATIONS, Ancillary, See Estates
ADMINISTRATOR, And Administratrix 77
ADOPTION, Internet Search Tools 31
ADOPTIONS, 47
ADULTERY, Varying Attitudes Toward 9
AFFINITY, Degrees Of 72
AGES, As Research Tools 47 Deduced From Censuses 41 Inferences Drawn From 47-48 Of Majority 48
AMERICAN COLONIES, 55
ANCESTORS, Elusive 2 Estates Of 75 Hard Times Of 68 Illiteracy Of 44 In Courts' Orders 79 Need For Certainty As To 2 Need For Government Nearby 34 Not To Be Judged 68 Tracing Title To Lands Of 65 Use Of Intoxicants By 44
ANCESTRAL HOME, Sketch From Civil War Book (illus.) 91
ANCILLARY ADMINISTRATIONS, See Estates 75
APPRAISEMENTS OF ESTATES, See Public Sales 79
APPRENTICE AND APPRENTICES, 44 In Tax Records 89
APPRENTICED, 44
ARCHIVES, At Battlefields And Shrines 61 Courthouses As 61 Family Collections Are 61 National Parks, Historic Sites, Depts Of Govt, As 61 Of States Veterans' Records In 19
ASSESSMENTS, 62
ASSESSOR, Tax 64
ASSETS, 64
ASSUMPTIONS, The Making Of 3
AUCTIONS, See Public Sales 79

AUNTS, 46 Remote Titles Of 46
AUTOMOBILE REGISTRATIONS, 1927 (illus.) 12
AUTOMOBILES, As Reminders For Older Men 11-12

B

BANKS, Early Were Unknown 67-68
BAPTISM RECORDS KEPT BY CHURCHES, 23
BAPTISMAL RECORD, English, Dated 1647 (illus.) 23
BEQUESTS, 77
BIBLES, Need To Examine Notes In 13 Writings In, As Proof 3
BIRTH CERTIFICATES, As Evidence 5 Where To Gain 49
BIRTH PARENTS, 47
BIRTH RECORDS, Early 31 Searchable On Internet 31
BIRTH RECORDS KEPT BY CHURCHES, 23
BIRTHS, Places Of, As Determined By Censuses 41-42 Years Of, As Determined By Censuses 41
BLACK SHEEP, (reprobates) 9
BLOOD, Related By 72
BOARDERS, See Live-ins And Boarders
BOND, 77
BONDS, 64 In Estates, Importance Of 77
BOOKS, Abstracts, Extracts, Compilations 37 As Evidence 4 How To Use 37 On Microfilm And Microfiche 40 Online 30 Wide Variety Of Available 37
BOUNDARIES, Political, Changing Nature Of 33 Political, Examples Of 34 State, County, Etc. 34
BOUNTY LAND RECORDS, 16 See Land Grants 23

BROTHER, Use Of Title 46
BUREAU OF LAND MANAGEMENT (BLM), 30

C

CALENDAR, Change From Julian To Gregorian (illus.) 28
CALL NUMBERS, In Libraries 57
CALL SLIPS, In Libraries 57
CAMERA, Need For, In Research 7
CAMERAS, Need For, In Research 7
CARETAKERS OF CEMETERIES, As Sources 26
CASSETTE RECORDERS, See Tape Recorders
CATALOGS IN LIBRARIES, Computerized 33 Use Of 33 57
CDs (Compact Discs) Found On The Internet 30
CEMETERIES, As Revealing Other Researchers 26 Caretakers Of, As Sources 26 General Consideration Of 7 24 26 Headstones In 24 26 Locating Records Of 24 Locations Of Graves In 24 Map Locations Of 24 Name Of, As Important 24 Sextons As Record Keepers Of 26
CENSUS RECORDS, On Internet 31
CENSUSES, 1850 And After 44 Before 1850 45 Birthplaces Stated In 42 Calculating Birth Years From 41 Dates Of Marriages Deduced From 42 Decennial 2 37 Differences In Data In 39 Enumerators Of 41 43 Errors In, As Known To All 44 Errors In, Some Sources Of 41 44 Forms For, Where To Procure 39 Fostered And Apprenticed Persons 44 General Facts Concerning 39 Heads Of Households In 39 45 Indexes To 40 Information Found In Various 39 Live-ins And Boarders In 44-45 Microfilm And Microfiche Copies Of 40 Migrations Deduced From Births In 42 Moving Backwards Through 42 Order Of Households, Importance 40 Order Of Persons Enumerated In 45 Pagination In 40 Persons Missing From 39 Reliability Of 43 Research Using Examples 39 Slaves And Servants In 39 Taken By States 39 41 Thinking About, As Necessary 43 Examples 40

CERTIFICATES, Birth 49 Death 49
CHAMBERS OF COMMERCE, As Map Sources 7
CHARACTER OF ANCESTORS, Not To Be Judged 9
CHATTEL MORTGAGES, 62
CHILDBEARING, As Clues To Marriages And Deaths 69 Early, Examples Of 69 Years Of 69
CHILDREN, Adopted, Fostered, Etc. 44 46 As Clues To Parents 56 Church Records Concerning 23 Fostered Out 44 46 Mortality Of Early 69
CHRISTENINGS, Records Kept By Churches 23
CHURCH HISTORIES, On Internet 31
CHURCH MEETINGS, Records Of 23
CHURCHES, 23 Cemeteries Of 24 Congregations Of 24 Early Attendance In 23 Inactive 24 Inactive, Records Of 24 Locations Of, As Important 24 Mormon, Facilities Of 58 Records Of 7 19 Records Of Children In 23 Records Of, Repositories Of 24 Sextons Of Cemeteries Of 26
CHURCHYARDS, As Providing Evidence 4
CIRCUIT COURT, 74
CIRCUIT COURTS, See Courts
CITATIONS, 86
CITATIONS OF SOURCES, 37
CITIES, Boundaries Of 33 Histories Of 52
CIVIL WAR, Anecdote Concerning 15
CIVIL WAR ERA MEDICAL DISCHARGE DOCUMENT, (illus.) 21
CIVIL WAR REGISTERS, Finding On Internet 29
CLAIMS, Of Citizens Against Governments, Records Of 19
CLEAR AND CONVINCING, See Evidence And Proof
CLEARKS OF COURTS, 65
CLERK TO THE COURT, 65
CLUBS, See Societies And Clubs
COLLATERAL LINES, (Branches) 13 42
COLONIAL AND COLONIES, American 55
COMMODITIES AS MONEY, See Money
COMMON PEOPLE, Records Of 1
COMMON PLEAS COURT, 74
COMMON PLEAS COURTS, See Courts

COMPUTER TECHNOLOGY, In Census Research 41
CONDUCT OF ANCESTORS, 9
CONFIRMATION RECORDS, Kept By Churches 23
CONFLICTING INFORMATION, Handling Of 9
CONGREGATIONS, See Churches
CONSANGUINITY, Degrees Of 72
CONSCRIPTION, See Draft
CONSIDERATION, In Deeds 72
CONTRACEPTIVES, As Being Unknown Early 69
CONTRACTS, Ages Of Entering Upon 58
COUNTIES, Boundaries Of 33 Engineers Of, As Map Sources 7 64 Genesis Of 35 37 Genesis Of, Finding On Internet 29 Genesis Of, Maps 37 Histories Of, Accuracy 52 Histories, information Found In 37 52 New, Reasons For Formation 34-35 Records Of, Effects Of Genesis On 35 Seats Of 34 Sizes Of 35 Surveyors Of, As Maps Sources 7 Tax Assessors Of 64
COUNTY ENGINEER, 64
COUNTY HISTORIES, 37
COUNTY SEAT, 34
COUNTY SEATS, See Counties
COUNTY SURVEYOR, 64
COURSES IN GENEALOGY, 1
COURT, Circuit 74 Common Pleas 74 Orphans 74 Superior 74 Supreme 74 Surrogate 74 Term 76
COURTHOUSES, Ancestors In Courts' Rulings 79 As Maps Sources 64 As Not Intimidating 64 Burned, Examples 62 Courts' Orders And Notes Books 79 Courts' Orders As Chronological 80 Death Records In 63 Federal, Use Of 62 83 Finding Records In 64 Good Manners In 75 86 Indexes In 62-63 Intents To Be Naturalized In 83 Keeping And Care Of Records In 86 Land Records In 64-65 Loose Papers In 82 Miscellaneous Records In 82 Naturalization Records In 83 Reasons For Records Of 62 Records In, As Unchanging 61 Records Of Lawsuits Found In 79 Records, Examples 62 Research Discoveries, Examples Of 62 Research In, As Enjoyable 62 Research In, Generally 61

COURTHOUSES, (cont.) Research In, Need For 62 Rules Pertaining To Records 61 Tax Records In 64 83 Types Of Records Found In 61
COURTS, Circuit 74 Clerks Of 79 Common Pleas 74 Entries In 79 Federal 62 83 Minutes Of 79 Names Of Various 74 Orders Of 79 Orphans' 74 Probate, See Estates; Quarter Sessions 76 Quarter Sessions Of 76 Superior 74 Supreme 74 Surrogate 74 Writings Of, As Evidence 5 Writings Of, When Indexed 79
COURTS' JOURNALS, 79
COURTS' MINUTES, 79
COURTS' ORDERS, 79
COUSINS, 1st, 2nd, etc 46 Degrees Of Cousinhood 46
CRIMINALS, As Early Settlers 55
CURRENCY, See Money
CUSTOMS AND HABITS, As Clues 14

D

DEATH CERTIFICATE, Dated 1956 (illus.) 52
DEATH CERTIFICATES, 49
DEATH RECORDS, Searchable On Internet 31
DEATHS, Causes Of 79 Certificates Of, Where To Gain 49 Determining Dates Of Early 76 Holographic Wills At 76 Intestate 71 Nuncupative Wills At 76 Records Of, As Kept By Churches 23 Records Of, See Estates; Testate 75
DEBT, Jailing For 68
DEBTORS' PRISONS, 68
DECEDENTS, 75 See Estates
DEED, Dated 1741/1742 (illus.) 28 Typical (illus.) 75
DEEDS, 64-65 As Evidence 4-5 Consideration In 72 Descriptions Of Land In 69 Distinguished From Mortgages 67 Dower Reflected In 69 Early, Importance Of 14 Formerly Not Needed At Death 67 How Indexed 65 Love And Affection In 72 Monies Stated In 72 Mortgage 65 Of Mortgage 65 Of Partition 65 Of Partition, Genealogical Value Of 71 Of Trust 65 67-68 Quit-Claims As 64 70 Residences Often Revealed In 70

DEEDS (cont.)
  Signed By Other Than Owners 67
  Spouses Found In 69 Unrecorded Or
  Missing 67 Warranty 65 69 Where
  Often Found 64
DEEDS OF PARTITION, 65 72
DEEDS OF TRUST, 62 65 68 See
  Mortgages
DEFINITIONS, Of Property 64
DEGREES OF AFFINITY, 72
DEGREES OF CONSANGUINITY, 72
DERIVATIVE SOURCES, 62
DESCENT AND DISTRIBUTION, 77 See
  Estates
DEVISE, 77 See Estates
DEVISES, 77
DIALECT, See Accents And Dialects
DIRECT INDEX, 65
DIRECT INDEXES, 65
DIRECTORIES, Courthouse, Use Of 65
  74 Genealogical, Addresses Of Select,
  See Appendix 3
DISCHARGE, Military 4
DIVORCE, Attitudes Toward 9
DOCUMENT, Certified Copy Of A 1760
  (illus.) 68
DOCUMENTS, Certified Copies Of 30
  Digitizing Of 30 Early, Importance Of
  13
DOMICILE, 77
DOWER, 70 See Deeds
DOWER INTERESTS, 69
DRAFT, 15 (conscription) 15
DUTCH PENNSYLVANIA, 59

E

ELIZABETHAN ENGLISH, 80
ELIZABETHAN STYLE ENGLISH, 80
ELLIS ISLAND, 30
ENGINEER, County 64
ENGINEERS, See Counties
ENGLISH, Early, Examples Of Characters
  80 Early, How To Read 80
ENUMERATIONS, 39
ENUMERATORS, Character Of 44 Errors
  By 43 Of Censuses 41 43 Sources Of
  Information Used By 44
ERRORS, In Censuses 44 In Other
  Records, What To Do 86
ESTATE RECORDS, See Estates
ESTATES, 48 Administrator And
  Administratrix 77

ESTATES (cont.)
  Ancillary Administrations In 75
  Appraisements/Appraisals In 77
  Bonds In 77 Decedents In 75 Descent
  And Distribution Statutes 76
  Determining Death Dates From 77
  Devises And Bequests Found In 77
  Early, Determining Death Dates From
  77 Execution Dates Of Wills In 76
  Executor And Executrix 76 Final
  Settlements And Orders In 76 79
  Holographic Wills In 76 Indexes To 75
  Intestate Deaths In 70 77 Inventories
  Of, Importance Of 77 Nuncupative
  Wills In 76 Per Stirpes Distributions
  In 79 Probating Of, Genealogical
  Value Of 76 Probating Of, Purposes 76
  Proving Of Wills In 76 Public Sales In,
  Importance 79 Recording Dates Of
  Wills 76 Records Of 64 75 Summaries
  Of Debts And Accounts 79 Sureties In
  77 Testate Deaths In 75 Witnesses In,
  Importance Of 76
EVIDENCE AND PROOF, Best Available
  Is Needed 4 Considered And
  Discussed 3 From Inferences 4
  Illustrations Of 3 Measures Of, As
  Subjective 5 Reliability Of 3
  Speculation, Conjecture, Guesses 3
  Tests And Standards 3 Weight To Be
  Given To 3
EXECUTION, Of A Will 76 Of Quit-Claims
  70
EXECUTOR, 75 Of A Will 76 See Estates
EXECUTRIX, 75 Of A Will 76 See Estates
  75
EXTRACTS, 37

F

FAMILY COLLECTIONS, 61 See Archives
FAMILY GROUP SHEET, See Forms 2
FAMILY HISTORY CENTERS, 58 Of The
  Mormon Church 58
FAMILY HISTORY CENTERS , LDS 31
FAMILY HISTORY LIBRARY CATALOG,
  LDS 31
FAMILY NAME FILES, 53-54 Reliability
  Of 53-54
FAMILY TALES AND TRADITIONS, See
  Tales And Traditions
FAMILY UNIT CHART, See Forms 2 Uses
  Of 48-49

FAMILY GROUP SHEETS, See Forms
FEDERAL COURTS, See Courthouses
FEMME SOLE, 85
FEMME SOLE TRADER, 85
FILM READERS, 57
FINAL ORDER, Distribution Of Assets 79
FINAL ORDERS, See Estates
FINAL SETTLEMENT, Of A Will 76
FINAL SETTLEMENTS, See Estates
FIVE-GENERATION PEDIGREE CHART,
    See Forms 2
FOODS, As Clues 14
FOREIGN ARCHIVES AND LIBRARIES,
    Searching On Internet 28
FOREIGN LANGUAGES, As Clues 14
FORMS, Census, Storage Of 2 Censuses
    37 Cesuses Examples 93 Example 93
    Family Unit Charts 2 9 93 Federal
    Censuses 2 Five Generation Pedigree
    2 93 Instructions For Copying
    Examples Of 93 Manner Of Storing 2
    NATF-80 15 109 NATF-81 110 NATF-
    82 110 Printed, Need And Use Of 2
    Where To Procure 2 37
FOSTERED OUT, 31 44 See Children
FOUNDLINGS, Research Concerning 47
FRATERNITIES AND SORORITIES, 22
    See Societies And Clubs
FREE PERSONS OF COLOR, As Taxable
    85
FUNERAL RECORDS, Use Of 24 49

G

GENEALOGISTS, And Family Historians,
    our Duties As 9
GENEALOGY, A Definition 3 Courses In
    1 Is Family History 1 The Writing Of
    87 Web Pages 28
GENESIS, Of Counties 37 Of Counties,
    Finding On Internet 29
GENESIS OF COUNTIES, 35 Effects On
    Records 35 Examples 35 How To Find
    35
GENESIS OF STATES, Maps Showing 37
    Mentioned 35
GIVEN NAME, 39
GIVEN NAMES, See Nicknames
GODPARENTS, 23
GOVERNMENT, Local 34 Local, Need For
    34
GRAND, (title) 46
GRANTEE, 65

GRANTEE INDEX, 65 See Deeds
GRANTOR, 65
GRANTOR INDEX, 65
GRANTORS INDEX, 65 See Deeds
GRANTS, 17
GRANTS OF LAND, As Assets 17
GRAVE MARKERS, 24
GREAT, (title) 46
GREAT SEAL OF THE UNITED STATES,
    17
GROUNDS KEEPERS, As Sources 26

H

HANDWRITING, Quill Pen 80
HARD TIMES OF ANCESTORS, 68
HEAD TAX, 85
HEADS OF HOUSEHOLDS, 39
HEADSTONES, 24 As Evidence 4
    Deterioration And Reading Of 26
    Primitive 26
HERITAGE BOOKS INC, 30
HISTORY, Need For Some Knowledge Of
    54
HOLOGRAPHIC WILLS, 76 See Estates
HOMESTEADING, 16
HOMESTEADS, And Homesteading 16
HORSES, Travel By 24
HOUSEHOLDS, Heads Of 39 Neighbors
    Of 40 Order Of Enumeration 45
IACOCCA, Lee 30

I

ILLEGITIMACY, Attitudes Toward 9
ILLITERACY, Of Ancestors 44
IMMIGRANTS, As Criminals 55
    Indentured Servants As 55 Lists Of,
    As Kept At National Archives 110
    Passenger Lists As Showing 56
    Redemptioners As 55 Some Periods Of
    Migrations Of 59
IMMIGRATION HISTORY CENTER, 30
IMMIGRATION INFORMATION, To Be
    Made Available On The Internet 30
INCHOATE RIGHTS, 69 See Dower
INDENTURED SERVANTS, 55
INDEX TO INTERMENTS, 26
INDEXES, Computerized 41 Early 65
    Grantee/Reverse 65 Grantor/Direct
    65 In Courthouses 64 Miscellaneous
    82 Of Mortgages 65 Soundex, Use Of
    41 To Censuses 40 To Estates, How
    Arranged 75

INFERENCES, As Evidence 4 47-48
INK, Poor Quality In Early Years 80
INSANITY, Statement Of (illus.) 10
INSTRUMENTS, 65
INTANGIBLE PROPERTY, 64
INTANGIBLES, 64
INTELLECTUAL INTEGRITY, As A Test Of
    Proof 5
INTENT TO BE NATURALIZED, 83
INTENT TO BE NATURALIZED, 83
INTER-LIBRARY LOAN, 58
INTER-LIBRARY LOAN SERVICES, 58
    See Libraries
INTERMENTS, Importance Of Records Of
    23 49 Indexes To 26 See Deaths
INTERNET, 27 As One Of Many
    Resources 27 32 As Tool For Research
    27 BLM Land Patent Records On 30
    Census Records On 31 Convenience
    Of 27 Immigration Information To Be
    Made Available On 30 Obtaining
    National Archives Records Via 15
    Researching Other Areas On 29
    Searching For Books On 29-30
    Searching Foreign Archives And
    Libraries On 28 Sharing Of
    Information Via 28-29 Surname
    Search On 28 Use Of E-mail 28-29
    Volunteer Projects On 29 What Can
    Be Found On 27
INTERNET SOURCES, Proper Reference
    Form 38
INTERVIEWS, 7 Commencement Of 9
    Dates Of, As Important 14 Good
    Manners In 9 How To Conduct 9
    Importance Of Past Residencies In 11
    Keeping Control Of 13 Learning Of
    Foreign Languages From 14 Need For
    Maps During 7 Planning For 7
    Questions During 9 Recorders Needed
    During 7 Sensitive Subjects In 9 Wars
    As Reminders During 15
INTESTATE, Death 75
INTESTATE DEATH, 71 Administrations
    Of Estates Of 76 See Estates
INTESTATE SUCCESSION, 79 See
    Estates
INTOXICANTS, Early Use Of 44
INVENTORIES, In Estates 77 See Estates
INVENTORY, 77
INVENTORY AND APPRAISAL, Of 1760
    Estate (illus.) 80

INVENTORY AND APPRAISEMENT, 77

J

JACKET, 75
JACKETS, 75 See Estates
JAILS, And Incarceration For Debt 68
JOURNALS, Of Courts 79
JR, (junior) 45
JUDGES, Entries Of Orders And Rulings
    Of 79 Orders And Entries, How To Use
    79 See Courts
JUDGMENTS, Of Ancestors, As Improper
    9
JURISDICTIONS, 75

K

KINFOLKS, As Lenders In Mortgages 68
    Degrees Of Kinship 72
KINSHIP, Degrees Of Consanguinity 72

L

LAND, Deeds And Documents
    Concerning 65 Descriptions Of 74
    Records In Courthouses 64 Tracing
    Title To 62
LAND GRANTS, 16 Early Sale Of 17 How
    Brought About 17 Making
    Assumptions From 19 Records Of
    Service Connected To 16 To Early
    Citizens 17 Utilization Of Early 19
LAND OFFICES, 17
LAND PATENT RECORDS, On Internet
    30
LAND RECORDS, States And Federal
    Government 17
LANDOWNER MAP, 1871 Township
    (illus.) 56
LANGUAGES, Foreign, As Clues 14
LATIN WORDS, In Legal Writings 65
LATTER DAY SAINTS, Church Of Jesus
    Christ Of 58 Church Of Jesus Christ
    Of See Mormons
LAWSUITS, Records Of 79
LDS, Microfilm Records Available 31-32
    Records On Internet 31 See Mormons
LDS FAMILY HISTORY CENTERS, 58
LDS LIBRARY, 33
LEGAL TERMS, Examples 65 In Deeds
    And Documents 65 Understanding 65
LETTERS/CORRESPONDENCE, Early,
    Importance Of 13
LIABILITIES, 64

LIBRARIES, 33 Call Numbers In 58 Call Slips In 57 Catalogs In 33 57 Census Records In 39 Courtesy While Using 33 Family Name Files In 53 Film Viewers In 57 Indexes In 33 Inter-library Loan Services Of 58 Local Materials To Be Found In 52 Major, Some 33 Microfilm And Microfiche In 57 Of States, Records Of Veterans In 19 Records Of Veterans In 19 Research In, Commencing 33 Research In, Methods And Examples 33 Research In, Prior Planning 33 Special, Some 33 Stacks In 57 What They Do 33

LIBRARY OF CONGRESS, Web Page 27

LIENEE, 65

LIENOR, 65

LIENS, 62

LINEAGE, Collaterial 13

LIST OF TAX-PAYERS, 1810 From County History (illus.) 55

LITIGATION, 79 See Courts; See Lawsuits

LIVE-INS AND BOARDERS, 44 In Censuses 44-45

LIVING MEMORIES, Need To Gain 7

LOOSE PAPERS, 82 Example Of, 1755 List Of Tithables Or Taxable Citizens 86 Example Of, 1755 Swearing In Of Constables (illus.) 84

LOVE, Early, As Not Necessary For Marriage 69

LOVE AND AFFECTION, As Consideration In Deeds 72

LUNACY RECORDS, 62

M

MAJORITY, 48

MANNERS, 89

MANORS, 34

MAP, (illus.) 38

MAPS, 7 As Revealing Genesis Of Counties 37 Churches Should Be Located On 23 Courthouses Have 64 Historical 64 Historical (illus.) 8 Importance And Procuring Of 7 Topos (USGS Quadrangles) 7 64

MARRIAGE BOND, 1773 (illus.) 73

MARRIAGE LICENSE, 1904 (illus.) 65

MARRIAGE RECORDS, Searchable On Internet 31

MARRIAGES, Clues To Records Of 43 Dates Of, Deduced From Censuses 42 Early 69

MEDICAL CARE, Early, Poor Quality Of 69

MEMENTOS, 9 As Reminders 9 Gathering Of Family 87-89

MEMORIES, Jogging Of, In Interviews 11 Of Living Relatives, Need To Gain 7

MICROFICHE, 57

MICROFILM, 57 And Microfiche 57 And Microfiche Use Of 57 And Microfiche, Censuses On 40 And Microfiche, Censuses On, Pagination 40 Pagination 40 Viewer 40

MICROFILM RECORDS, Available From LDS 31-32

MIGRATIONS, Examples 57 Of Ethnic Groups 40 Of Neighbors And Church Groups 40 Westward 56 59

MILITARY, Service Records Of, As Important 14

MILITARY HISTORY, Via USAMHI Web Site 32

MILITARY MOVEMENTS, Records Of 15

MILITARY UNITS, Lists Of, On Internet 29

MILITIA, Units Of, Service In 19

MISCELLANEOUS INDEX, 82

MISCELLANEOUS RECORDS, 82

MONEY, 72 As Clue To Residency 72 As Commodity 72 As Negotiable Instrument 72 Forms Of 73

MORALITY, Attitudes Toward 9

MORMON FAMILY HISTORY CENTERS, 58

MORMON LIBRARY, 33

MORMONS, Records On Internet 31

MORMONS (LDS), Facilities And Services Of 31 58

MORTGAGE DEEDS, 65

MORTGAGEE, 65 67

MORTGAGES, 62 67 Chattel 62 Distinguished From Deeds 68 Indexing Of 68 Kinfolks Often Held 68 Reasons For 68 Releases Of 68

MORTGAGOR, 65 67

MOURNING CARD, Dated 1890 (illus.) 25

MOVEMENTS, Of Ancestors, as Shown In Deeds 67

MOVEMENTS, Of Groups 40

MR AND MRS, As Titles 47

N

NAMES, Changes Of, Reasons For 44
Recurrent, Importance Of 42
NARA, E-mail Address 15 How To Obtain
Copies Of Records From 15 National
Archives And Records Administration
15 Website Address 15
NATF-80, 29
NATIONAL ARCHIVES, 15 22 Mailing
Address Of 15 Record Of Civil War
Service Found In 29 Records Of
Veterans' Widows 19 Regional System,
How To Use 111-112 Web Site
Address 15
NATIVITY, 42
NATURALIZATION, 83
NATURALIZATION RECORDS, 83 As
Available From National Archives 112
NEGOTIABLE INSTRUMENTS, 73 See
Money
NEIGHBORS, Of Ancestors, Importance
Of Noting 40
NEWSLETTERS, See Periodicals
NEWSPAPERS, As Evidence 5 As
Research Tools 52 Early, Use Of 13
Reliability Of 53 Where To Find Early
52
NEXT OF KIN, 79
NICKNAMES, Wide Use Of, Early 46
NOTE TAKING, In Interviews 7
NOTES, Promissory 64
NUNCUPATIVE WILLS, 76 Witnesses In
76

O

OBITUARIES, As Sources 52
OBITUARY, 13 52
OBITUARY NOTICE, From 1827
Newspaper (illus.) 90
OCCUPATIONS, Of Ancestors,
Determining Of, From Estate Files 79
OF AGE, 48
OLD COUNTRIES, Research Concerning
56
ORDER BOOKS, 79 See Courts
ORIGINAL RECORDS, 61
ORPHANS COURT, 74
ORPHANS COURTS, See Courts
OUTCRY, Sale By 79

P

PARTITION, Deeds Of 65 72
PASSENGER LISTS, As Available At
National Archives 110 Of Ships 56
PASTORS (PREACHERS), As Sources Of
Information 23
PATERNAL, 45
PEDIGREE, Five Generation, See Forms
PENNSYLVANIA DUTCH, See Dutch
PENSION APPLICATIONS, 16
PENSIONS, Of Early Veterans 17
PER, Stirpes See Estates
PER STIRPES, 79
PERIODICALS, 54 Addresses Of Select
114 Genealogical 51 54 Of Counties
And Areas 52 Of Families 52 Of States
And Nationalities 51
PERSONAL PROPERTY, 64 85
PERSONALTY, 64 85
PETITION, 1723, With Names Of Area
Residents (illus.) 62
PHONETIC NAME SPELLING, By
Enumerators 44
PHONETIC SPELLING, In Early
Documents 44
PHOTOGRAPH, Ancestor (illus.) 14
PHOTOGRAPHS, Finding Historic 32
Historic, copies Available Via Internet
32
PHOTOS, As Reminders 9 Dating Of, Is
Important 13 Early, Value Of, As
Evidence 9 13 Gaining, To Make
Copies Of 9
POLITICAL SUBDIVISIONS, 33
POLL TAX, 85
POLL TAXES, 85
POLLS, 85
POVERTY, As Pension Requirement 17
PREACHERS (PASTORS), As Sources Of
Information 23
PRECINCTS, 34
PREDECESSOR COUNTIES, 37
PREPONDERANCE OF EVIDENCE, See
Evidence And Proof
PRESIDENT OF THE US, Sometimes
Signed Land Grants 17
PRIESTS, As Sources Of Information 23
PRIMARY SOURCES, 4
PRIMOGENITURE, 70
PROBATE ACTIVITY, See Estates
PROBATE COURT RECORD, Statement
Of Insanity (illus.) 10

PROBATE RECORDS, 74 See Estates
PROFESSIONAL RESEARCHERS, 52
    Credentials Of 52
PROMISSORY NOTES, 64
PROOF, See Evidence And Proof
PROPERTY, Intangible 64 Personal 64
    Real 64 Tangible 64 Taxes Levied
    Against 83 85
PROTHONOTARY, 72
PROVE, A Will 76
PROVING OF WILLS, See Estates
PUBLIC OFFICES, Early, Desirability Of
    47
PUBLIC RECORDS, 61
PUBLIC SALES, Of Estates 79 See
    Estates

Q

QUADS (TOPOS), 64 See Maps
QUARTER SESSIONS, See Courts
QUARTER SESSIONS COURTS, 76
QUERIES, 51
QUESTIONS, To Relatives 9
QUILL PENS, Early Writing With 44
QUIT-CLAIMS, 65 70 Example Of Uses
    70 Genealogical Value Of 70 See
    Deeds

R

READER, See Viewer
REAL ESTATE, 62 64
REAL PROPERTY, 64
REALTY, 64
RECIPES, As Clues To Residency 14
RECOLLECTIONS, Of Relatives 7
RECORDING, Of Deeds, see Deeds
RECORDS, Apprentices In Tax 85 Care
    And Keeping Of 86 Courthouse, As
    Unchanging 61 Courthouse,
    Examples Of 62 Courthouse, Indexing
    Of 62 Early Written, As Unchanging
    61 Early Written, Examples Of Letters
    80 Early Written, How To Read 80
    Estate, how Indexed 75 Gathering Of
    Family 87 Importance Of Making
    Copies Of 52 In Federal Courthouses
    83 Indexes Of Tax 86 Intents To Be
    Naturalized, Finding 83 Keeping Of, as
    Necessary 1 Left By Ancestors 1 Loose
    Papers As 82 Miscellaneous 82
    Naturalization, Where To Find 82
    Numbers Of Persons From Tax 85

RECORDS, Of Naturalization, Finding 83
    Of Taxes And Assessments 83 Public,
    Use Of 61
REDEMPTIONERS, 55
REFERENCES, Proper Form 38
REGISTERS OF DEEDS, 65
REGISTERS/REGISTRARS, 65 See
    Courthouses
REGISTRAR, 65
RELATIVES, Methods Of Questioning Of
    9 Need To Interview 7 Planning
    Interviews Of 9 Reviving Memories Of
    11
RELEASE OF MORTGAGE, How
    Recorded 67
REMOVED, (Once, Twice, Etc.) 46
REPROBATES, (Black Sheep) 9
RESEARCH, By Professionals 52 Finding
    Others Engaged In 51 Forms Helpful
    In 93-108 How To Use Books In 37 In
    Courthouse 62 Of Old Countries 56
    Outside Home Counties 75 Periodicals
    As A Tool For 54 Planning For Library
    58 Reliability Of Others Doing 51
    Time Line Drawings As Aid To 48
    Westward Movements As Tools For 59
    With Local Materials 52
RESIDENCIES OF ANCESTORS,
    Methods Of Determining 24
REUNIONS, Family, Importance Of 13
REVERSE INDEX, 65
REVERSE INDEXES, See Grantee
REVOLUTIONARY WAR ERA
    DOCUMENT, (illus.) 18
REVOLUTIONARY WAR SOCIETIES, 22
ROSTERS MILITARY, Found On Internet
    29
RULES, For Research In Courthouses 61

S

SASE, 51
SEARCH ENGINES, 27 45
SECONDARY SOURCES, 4
SERVANTS AND SERVITUDE, In
    Censuses 39 Indentured And
    Otherwise 55
SETTLERS, Early, Poverty Of 55
    Research Tools As To 55
SEXTON, 26
SEXTONS, Records Of 26
SHIPS LISTS OF PASSENGERS, As Tools
    56

SIBLINGS, 42 See Collateral Lines
SISTER, Use Of Title 46
SKEPTICISM, Need For, In Genealogical Research 4
SLAVES, Knowledge Gained Of, In Censuses 39
SOCIETIES, Revolutionary War 22
SOCIETIES AND CLUBS, 22 Addresses Of Select 113 Genealogical, Memberships In 51 Names Of Some Select 22
SORORITIES AND FRATERNITIES, 22 Memberships In, As Research Tools 22
SOUNDEX, 41
SOUNDEX INDEXING SYSTEM, 41
SOURCES, Citing 37 Proper Citing Of 38
SPELLING, Of Names, Soundex 41 Of Surnames, Variations In 45 Phonetic 44
SPINSTER, 44
SPINSTERS, 45
SPONSORS OF CHILDREN, 23
SPOUSES, As Signatories In Deeds 69 Dower Of 69 Existence Of, As Shown In Deeds 69 Named In Warranty Deeds 69
SR (SENIOR), 45
STACKS, See Libraries
STATES OF BEING, Evidentiary 3
STATES OF THE UNION, Boundaries Of 33 Censuses Of 41 Vital Statistics Of 49
STOCK, Corporate 64
STONES, As Grave Markers 25
SUMMARIES, Of Debts And Accounts In Estates, Importance Of 79
SUPERIOR COURT, 74 See Courts
SUPREME COURT, 74 See Courts
SURETIES, 77 79
SURNAME, 39
SURNAMES, 37 45 As Keys To Periodicals 53 Importance In Overseas Research 56 Origins Of, As Important 45 Origins Of, Determining 44 Searching On Internet 28 Spelling Variations In 45
SURROGATE COURT, 74
SURROGATE COURTS, See Courts
SURVEYOR, County 64
SURVEYORS, As Sources For Maps 7 County, See Counties

T

TALES AND TRADITIONS, Family 4 Family, Importance And Reliability Of 26
TANGIBLE PROPERTY, 64
TANGIBLES, 64
TAPE/CASSETTE RECORDERS, In Interviews 7
TAX ASSESSOR, 64
TAX ASSESSORS, See Counties
TAX OFFICES, As Sources Of Maps 7
TAX RECORDS, In Courthouses 64
TAX ROLLS, 83
TAXES, Apprentices In Lists Of 85 Free Persons Of Color 85 Indexing Of Records Of 86 Inferences Fairly Drawn From 83 Levied Against Whom 83 Numbers Of Persons From Lists Of 85 Records Of 83
TERM, Of Court 76
TERMS, Legal, Examples 65
TERMS OF COURT, Value Of Knowing 76
TESTATE, Death 75
TESTATE DEATH, 75 See Estates
TESTIMONY, For A Will 76
THREE RING BINDERS, Need For 2
TIME LINE DRAWINGS, 48
TITHABLE, 48 85
TITHE, 85
TITHES AND TITHABLES, 85
TITLE, In Property 67
TITLE TO LAND, Tracing Of 67
TITLES, Mr. And Mrs. 47 Of Honor 47 Of Public Officials 47 Sr. And Jr. 46
TOPOS, See Maps
TOPOS (QUADS), Usgs 7 Usgs (illus.) 8
TOWNSHIPS, Changing Boundaries 33
TRADITIONS, See Tales And Traditions
TRAVEL, Early 24 On Horseback Or Foot 35
TRUST, Deeds Of, See Deeds

U

U S MILITARY HISTORY INSTITUTE, 32
UNCLES, 46 Remote, Titles Of 46
US ARMY MILITARY HISTORY INSTITUTE, History Availabe Via Web Site 32
USGS QUADRANGLES, 7-8 See Maps 7

V

VEHICLES, Reminders For Older Men 11
VELLUM, 17
VENDEE, 65
VENDOR, 65
VERTICAL FILES, 53
VETERANS, 7 15 Bounty Lands Awarded To 16 Dependents Of, Benefits For 16 Forms To Gain Records Of 15 Land Grants Awarded To 16 Pension Records Of 15 Poverty Of Some Early 17 Records At National Archives 109-110 Records Of Categories Of 15 Records Of Widows Of 16 Records Of, Generally 15 Records Of, In Libraries 19 Service In Militias 19 Warrants For Land Granted To 17 Widows Of, Pension 19
VETERANS' RECORDS, 17 Locations 19 Revolutionary War 17
VETERANS DISCHARGES, 4
VIEWERS (READERS), For Microfilm And Microfiche 40
VITAL INFORMATION, Laws Concerning Preservation Of 31
VITAL STATISTICS, 49
VITAL STATISTICS OF STATES, As Research Tools 49
VOLUNTEER PROJECTS, On Internet 29

W

WARRANTS, For Land 17
WARRANTY DEEDS, 65 69 See Deeds
WARS, Claims For Non-military Service 19 Early Service In, As Reminders 11 Families Involvements In 15 Interview Questions Concerning 11 Service During Early, As Evidentiary 15
WARTIME CLAIMS, See Wars
WEB PAGES, Genealogy 28
WESTWARD MIGRATIONS, 56 59
WIDOW, As Femme Sole 85 Of Veteran, Pension And Benefits Of 16
WIDOWS PENSION, From National Archives (illus.) 20
WILL, 1678, Example Of Document That Is Difficult To Read (illus.) 83
WILLS, Action Of 76 Executors And Executrixes Of 76 Holographic 76 Nuncupative 76 Proving Of 76 Recording And Executions, Dates Of 76 See Estates
WITNESSES, In Church Ceremonies 23 In Litigation 79 To Deeds 69 To Wills 76
WORLD WIDE WEB, 27
WRITING, Early English 80 Of Family Histories 87 Quality Of Ink 44 Reading 80 With Quill Pens 44

About the Authors

Paul Drake, J.D., has degrees in history and law and has been doing genealogical and historical research for forty-five years. An accomplished and recognized lecturer and teacher at Roane State College and, formerly, at Tennessee Technical University, Dr. Drake has written two books and numerous articles concerning the Civil War, historical research and evidence, and genealogy (for both the beginning and the advanced researcher), which have been published in various state and national journals.

Ms. Driskill, an active Social Worker, teaches Genealogy at the University of Alabama, Huntsville. She portrays in first person Abigail Smith Adams for schools and civic groups, presenting the role of women during the American Revolutionary War.

www.ingramcontent.com/pod-product-compliance
Lightning Source LLC
Chambersburg PA
CBHW080615270326

41928CB00016B/3072